THIRTY
DAYS
—OF—
THOUGHT

CULTURE MATTERS

JAY DORAN

Editor: Jenna Silverman

jay@culturemattersllc.com

YOU ARE NOT ONLY WRITING YOUR
BOOK– YOU ARE WRITING YOUR LIFE
CULTURE . UNITES . AUTHORS

CULTURE UNITES AUTHORS

Authors Unite and Culture Matters Collaboration

**BELIEF
PURPOSE
GOAL
VISION
MISSION**

YOU ARE NOT ONLY WRITING YOUR
BOOK– YOU ARE WRITING YOUR LIFE
CULTURE . UNITES . AUTHORS

Belief: We believe that when people write a book with meaning, their legacy lives on.

AUTHORS
UNITE

Purpose: To guide people through writing their own book.

Goal: To make writing fun so people develop themselves through the written word.

**CULTURE
MATTERS**

Vision: To live in a world where people are excited to write.

Mission: To create experiences around writing.

Culture Unites Authors
An Authors Unite and Culture Matters collaboration

Culture Unites Authors was born at the precipice of an idea over-looking an entire industry, the personal development industry or human culture. The idea that in a world where everyone has a voice, they also are imbued with the knowledge that they hold the power to that voice. When obtaining the proper tools, guidance and knowledge people can grow themselves through their writing. Culture Unites Authors believes that when the individual writes their book with meaning, their legacy lives on forever. Families will learn from their ancestors and children do become parents; the leaders of the future. Through Culture Unites Authors, experiences are created around writing for people to grow through their writing to become authors who change the world. The collaboration between Culture Matters and Authors Unite was a perfect storm that has resulted in a rainbow and at its end is your next book. The book published by Culture Unites Authors is the one you write for your personal growth and with your growth the world will be better for it.

Please visit cultureunitesauthors.com to send us your information.

TABLE OF CONTENTS

DIRECTIONS FOR FILMING YOUR ONE MINUTE VIDEO

1

HOOK
(FROM 0-3 SECONDS)

Capture their attention immediately, so no video bumper, saying your name, or reusing what you might have in a TV spot.

2

IGNITE PAIN/ PLEASURE
(FROM 3-15 SECONDS)

Users must identify with the problem or opportunity. Ask a question, show success or failure. make clear the benefit.

3

DESCRIBE SOLUTION
(FROM 15-50 SECONDS)

What are you offering, what is the product or service?

4

CALL TO ACTION
(FROM 50-60 SECONDS)

What do you want them to do?

Dennis Yu, CEO, BlitzMetrics

PREFACE

This is not anyone's book but your own. Use this as what it is, a tool. Every day, read, write and speak to develop your truth and serve others through your development. Over thirty days you will write your book, your content, your course, your value and through that you will create more meaning in your life and others. This book is a launch pad for your book. As you use this as yours your light will shine bright. This is yours because your culture matters.

INTRODUCTION

THE DARK

From the great abyss comes light, and out of the void of nothing presents something, whether good or evil. Regardless of your morality, the creed you live by, the God you worship, or others you may pray for we must respect one thing- the decision made upon a thought. Now consider this, your thoughts subdue or propel your being into action or inaction. This book that has presented itself in your hands, whether by another or due to another cause, (there are no coincidences) has meaning behind it and its meaning will be determined by two things: one, the genetic compilation of every one of your cells, call this your DNA, and two, an effect of the environment you are a determinate of. In this moment, you will both read it and see it as a sign to keep digging and diving into your soul of future possibility or as danger, and you will thrust it down in contempt. Either effect is fine, and one will occur, but both are determined by the former casualties and inevitably only one thing matters, that you had the opportunity to choose and a decision was made.

This brings us to why this text was transcribed in the first place. In its raw form the answer is to prepare you for battle. No, not a physical battle but an inner conflict with your greatest foe; yourself. Within the confines of your physical form lies the only enemy that could ever devastate you to your very being. This creature has many shapes, symbolic representations and goes by a platitude of names, but it's easiest to refer to him or her as the dark. The dark is here now as you read, interpret and reflect upon this text. It is the whispering voice of doubt, of curiosity, and the questioning of purpose. The dark hawks our every movement until our physical death. The dark is both friend and foe and we are not here to silence the dark but to enable it. Although common myth would beg an immoral conception of any symbol represented in darkness to be ill or unadvised, we beg to differ. The dark is your future, your past and the present all at once. The dark is your power, it is your thoughtful essence. The dark is the bridge between what is, what could be and what you want it to be. This text is meant to evoke the dark into a position of power and enable you to take control. The dark is to drive forth your personal power and call for the beauty within yourself and to utilize your gifts of imagination. The dark is to quell the voices of doubt from the mechanical side of your mind, the limiting you, the you meant to create balance that destroys your creativity and stunts your dark companion of development. The dark is your articulation, your speech, your thought, it is the driving force for all innovation for the good that has come about in this world of man. The dark is where genius lies between the recognition of pattern and imagination. The dark is what we tap into when we lift the pen and place it to parchment, and just let go. The dark is where we go when we are the source of our competency. It is the place of power we operate from when we speak our word, without script and without pre-ordained cognition. There is no falsehood that resides in the dark, only truth. The dark is the origin of light and without harvesting the dark our light of creation can never come into being.

This text is meant to disturb, to evoke, to inspire and cause you to weep in comprehension of what has been written hitherto, so your inner soul may come into light through the dark- that hidden sound of questioning that you have done so good of trying to keep silent. In the dark lies the conductivity of thought and in that act lays our hidden source of power. Our mind is the invisible net of thought; universal collective unconscious woven together into imagination, grabbing the light so it may shine forth. What is light? Light is love, the truth of humanity lies in our decision to accept all for what is, as it is, and only through thought can we define our soul, and ration our behavior. Only through thought can we actualize ourselves and create all that can be created out of darkness. Only through light can we become self-aware to harness the dark fully. This text is your first tool to gain your personal power; this dance of light and dark is where absolutes may be born. This book is a tool and should be used to harness the dark and shine your light. Read each selected text and use it as a foundation for your word, both written and spoken. Use this text as a slab of meat to feed your soul, and a foe to battle against if need be. These excerpts are not meant to be your truth, but only cause your truth to come forth. We challenge you to read them, write and speak your truth prior to moving on. This text is meant as it has been stated, a catalyst, nothing more and nothing less, provocative in its erudition but simple in its use. Use the following words to ignite your hidden flame, to erupt the darkness from within and bring your light forth in the shining of new ideas, actions and results in our world. Hidden between lies are the newly aggravated opinions, thoughts, and ideas your future may hold after contemplation. Grapple with what you feel, think and believe now. In this moment, write something, agree and disagree. For truth is yours to create, your argument is well taken and therefore loved.

The next thirty days are just the beginning of your journey into the darkness. It is time to decide, the fork presents itself unconscious slavery or freedom. The choice is yours; it is time for thirty days of thought. Start your journey of reading, writing and speaking daily. Come into the dark and bring forth your light.

LIFE LESSON

Best way to f*ck it all up? Argue and combat all while defending against the haters. Think of a negative comment like a cancer; when it grows in the comment section and grows when engaged with any retort other than love, understanding and acceptance. Not only does it grow, but it spreads negative meaning others will chime in and feed off of. Remember, people see life through their lens; they are the writer, producer, director and leading role in their life's movie. You are an extra according to them, and you need to own that. These are the majority; the mice and they will feed on self-hate because it's what they know. A mouse does not know the hunt, the mouse does not seek out the hunt, and the mouse does not seek out prey nor own their game. They do not know that language, they know gossip, and they scavenge and prey on the lions kill, on your kill. It was Nietzsche who said, "A lion is not angered over a mouse, his relative power is too great, defensiveness betrays weakness." A mouse sees what a mouse sees, and a lion sees what a lion sees. This is a truth of life- the opposite of what we know is also true and once we accept this truth, we can accept people and win them over…eventually. This truth is that we have already won over who matters. Ourselves.

"The opposite of what we know is also true." – Life Lesson

_____

_____

_____

_____

_____

_____

_____

_____

_____

_____

_____

_____

_____

_____

_____

_____

_____

Do not forget to film a video!

LABELS LIMIT

To label is to limit. Limitations are the non-physical chains of mediocrity with scarcity bias for lack of the antiquated, instinctual architecture of an imperfect, non-linear evolution of self. How have we arrived in this place of existence? We are not sure, but our personal power knows no bounds. We may argue a myriad of perspectives on the topic, however, only the truth that our ability to thwart our intentions with limiting beliefs is a blessed curse. I say blessed because it comes with untold power and even greater responsibility. Our boundless energy may be funneled through our self, and our self needs no label, it just is. I chose the word, "curse" because the potential of being so infinite is just that- infinite. As we evolve into our true self, we want answers and although we may never receive them, this is our world, this is purgatory. Regardless of the chosen view, labels will limit you. As water fills a jar, any lid that may be placed on top will cut off the expansive over flow of the water. We are water. Our mass is water. Water is life. We are life. Energy is life. Therefore, to label us is to place metaphorical lids on our state of being. All great leaps of consciousness and followed manifestation of physical material advancement are catapulted into existence by organisms who were one with self. Therefore, they had no lid. Their alignment with self and their personal power is infused into the culture around them as clues necessary to make this assertion. Labels limit as specialization kills curiosity. Curiosity breeds intelligence and intelligence is the bridge from the unknown to the known and instinct to spirit. We are but non-physical energy temporarily composed of physical construct. Our labels limit our advancement and advancement is life. Don't take my observation for granted. Study the world around you, the stars, the sky and you will find you are opening your eyes to beauty. Words may not describe only limit. When we focus on the sound, we come to find this truth is self-evident; labels limit.

"Our boundless energy may be funneled through our self, and our self needs no label, it just is." – Labels Limit

_____

_____

_____

_____

_____

_____

_____

_____

_____

_____

_____

_____

_____

_____

_____

_____

Do not forget to film a video!

MOM

Her auburn hair with the smell of love, her speech and tender embrace, I remember us. When we took time for talking, when we said, "I love you" to each other, and I know how much time has passed since we have done each of those things. Where does the world go when you're staring life in the face, yet blind to what's so clearly in front of you.

LOVE

RESPECT

APPRECIATION

GRATITUDE

You were there through everything. After fear and before victory you never left, but I never arrived. Eventually cut off and lost in translation we were two people with no frequency, but you never left. Love in my head and adrenaline in my veins, the struggle is day-by-day and constantly feels like I am trying to grab something that is completely unobtainable. My revelation is that it is in fact, unconditional love from you that I never accepted.

Well, I love you too, Mom.

"Where does the world go when you're staring life in the face, yet blind to what's so clearly in front of you." – Mom

"Where does the world go when you're staring life in the face, yet blind to what's so clearly in front of you." - Mom

_____

_____

_____

_____

_____

_____

_____

_____

_____

_____

_____

_____

_____

_____

_____

_____

_____

Do not forget to film a video!

Refer to page i for directions

Keep reading!
Keep writing!
Keep Filming!

DON'T FORGET TO FILM YOUR VIDEO!

Tag us when you're done!
 Culture Matters
 cultureunitesauthors

#thirtydaysofthought
#culturematters
#readwritespeak
#cultureunitesauthors

CARPE DIEM

Seize every day but grapple with what is to be focused on now and you shall be set free. Your destiny will become real and rooted in truth with proper execution. The year happens not in one idea, but on the fleeting thoughts that excite us and drive us. It is our perceived free will, that of decision that will cause our year to be rich or poor. To win our lives back from unconscious slavery we must take the year and break it down to the quarter. Take the quarter and divide it into months, then adjust the month to a week and a week to a day. Ah, carpe diem, seize the day by the suns motion and use your gravitational purpose. Capitalize on each face be it high or low by the hour. Clasp the hour by the minute and the second by each moment, and now you have the formula for success, do not wait or procrastinate. Success does not show up; it is a process of your decisions. Decision does not exist in the here and now. It is determined by your past development and it is your unconscious thought that drives your conscious behaviors today. What you decide today effects your next decision tomorrow. Therefore, to seize the day you must do your homework, Latin prose generally means the root for most profundity and that is our lesson today, internalize "Carpe Diem" and seize the day!

"Success does not show up; it is a process of your decisions." – Carpe Diem

_____

_____

_____

_____

_____

_____

_____

_____

_____

_____

_____

_____

_____

_____

_____

_____

Do not forget to film a video!

THE LAWS OF MAN

The laws of man hold no meaning but the meaning we infuse within them. The IV drip of purpose that's attached to every condition, constraint and permission we abide by or rebel against. This purpose will empower us, or this purpose will devour us. The "us" are the common folk; you, me, our neighbors and our friends. We are in this world together and it is our duty to make amends with it.

The laws of man hold no meaning except the individual meaning we place inside them. It's the prideful, the fearful, those full of anger and regret, the shameful, the guilty and the apathetic civility that deem this necessary. The command of arbitrary laws bestowed on generations of men who were given no choice. The freedom to choose the state of their being is a right only our higher force has been granted the power to bestow. Regardless of faith, creed or rank this force we speak of signifies the beginning. The unwavering truths that we are born with free will, the will to decide, think and act regardless of law. These laws of man hold no meaning, but the fire we spark within them will perhaps be used to spark freedom. The laws of man should not hold weight over love, peace and joy. The values that we are all gifted in some form are values to empower ourselves and to come to agreements with each other. Before we can create any law for anything, we must be present. Our decision to love verse hate, to take courage over pride, to choose to be calm over anger etc. shows the weight of our laws and the label of our existence.

"The laws of man hold no meaning except the individual meaning we place inside them." – The Laws of Man

_____

_____

_____

_____

_____

_____

_____

_____

_____

_____

_____

_____

_____

_____

_____

_____

Do not forget to film a video!

Self-Culture Can Influence and Create Culture

It is the character of man that determines our collective morality. Our every moment and the construct of our mind decide our present whether filled with beauty or torn apart and emptied by hate. Self-culture is each of our identifying characteristics that shape who we are, what we do and the words we say. Influence comes from our character and is an agreement between two self-cultures or two separate and equal men and women of character.

At every turn of conversation, we are either driving to our destination side by side or we are on two completely different paths of life.

Regardless of our self-culture surrounded by detours, filled with distraction based on our influence, our path must maintain smooth. The culmination of our character traits and how we represent them with our words, tone and speech effect how we influence our counter parts and determine where both parties lie on that path. Where ever we go, we are. Who we are will confirm in our actions and the impact we have on others. Therefore, our character or internal self-culture will always coexist with abstract cultures in general.

Culture is defined as a metaphorical ecosystem of shared belief created by an influencer and maintained by the alignment of the influenced. Pending on where we are in our lives to share our self-culture or character by any transcription or in conversation will ultimately determine if we are the influencer or the influenced. To step into our eternal and everlasting state of "one" we must define our narrative. To do so, we must articulate our character and/or our self-culture. Once we have articulated our culture, the ladder of life becomes one step less because we have separated the option to be influential instead of only being influenced. Our self-culture will create culture because culture needs more than one, and we are all apart of each other's story, editing each other's scripts and making everyone around us stronger. Whether you see that as good or bad is up to you.

"To step into our eternal and everlasting state of "one," we must define our narrative." - Self-Culture Can Influence and Create Culture

_____

_____

_____

_____

_____

_____

_____

_____

_____

_____

_____

_____

_____

_____

_____

_____

Do not forget to film a video!

Refer to page i for directions

Keep reading!
Keep writing!
Keep Filming!

DON'T FORGET TO FILM YOUR VIDEO!

Tag us when you're done!
f Culture Matters
📷 cultureunitesauthors

#thirtydaysofthought
#culturematters
#readwritespeak
#cultureunitesauthors

Frustrated

How is one perturbed by another when that which upsets him is his own duty- undeveloped, unearned and unexecuted upon? One cannot project unto others the falseness of his being juxtaposed between an angel on his left and demon on his right. The being, a day laborer of responsibility must have courage- at least enough to break themselves in. For without bearings no person can withstand the gravity of another's decision. One cannot control every outcome, one can only test their fate by their decision to work by developing their senses, all six of them, culture included. Therein lies one's mortality in the blunderings of their unconscious habituation. If one does not reflect on their actions, then they cannot tap into their senses completely. Touch, smell, taste, see, hear and culture, the sixth sense is culture because everyone should have inner alignment of their character. When one is not clear, one's weakness will reign through and gravity will take place. A better nature and worse evil are attracted at the same time and one's superpower and kryptonite will combine revoking their opportunity to step into their "higher self." At that moment, resentment or inner peace will be presented, and it will be up to a decision. The solution to frustration is inner peace. Stargazing confuses the senses, but mirrors show us our truth. Face your frustration with your reflection and take responsibility.

One cannot project unto others the falseness of his being juxtaposed between an angel on his left and demon on his right. – Frustrated

_____

_____

_____

_____

_____

_____

_____

_____

_____

_____

_____

_____

_____

_____

_____

_____

Do not forget to film a video!

FREE WILL

As free as a chained lion who knows no world outside of the cage, he reins King over. His dimensional awareness is limited by his view of life. To King lion he believes he is the master of his universe; the ruler of his jungle, master of his cage who knows no other environment, but only the one he has laid claim over. He believes he has free will, but only as free as his will may deem him and his will is but a passenger to his perspective. For it is the lion's perspective that charts his course. Every decision he makes and all the cognition he interprets is at the will of his bias perspective. If his perspective is shaped by the only environment he knows, his cage, then how can he have free will? The lion may feel free, and he may even be free, but he cannot know what he does not know. He is ignorant due to rational understanding; reality. The lion is caged, and for him, due to circumstance, the perspective knows no other circumstance therefore this may be his only judge of freedom. This lion, King of his only known jungle- this cage, with its bars so thin that they cannot even be seen by the naked eye, yet once noticed they may not be unseen, for this is awareness. All the choices the lion makes, and every freedom the lion acts upon seems to be that of his own accord. But who is to say that our lions will has not solely been shaped by perspective? This perspective driven by his probable circumstance; his genetics engaged inside his caged environment; he knows no other view. His free thought is that of itself, free, but who is to say so? After all, if every thought, idea and action is the effect of this cause, the environment around this lion, then how can he truly be free? His biggest albatross may be his belief in freedom. In full respect for his Kingship he is but a slave to his own belief of freedom, the perfect slave. An organism so enslaved he is convinced he is the King of *his* jungle. When his jungle is solely an illusion of his mind, and our lions mind is but a slave to the circumstances that surround it, how they become perceived is based on factors our lion cannot control. Our universe has a sick sense of humor, one that thinks it is funny to perceive anyone of having free will when in reality it is determined by our environment. Our environment is just a statistical probability of rocks banging into other rocks to birth stars shining on other stars. This cycle of life goes on with or without free will. The perfect slave is God, a King and a slave. The apparent hierarchy juxtaposes better or worse or free or not free. Therefore, that is a question never to be answered. However, let us create one together and be sure to write and speak what you believe. For that is the answer that matters.

"He believes he has free will, but only as free as his will may deem him and his will is but a passenger to perspective." – Free Will

_____

_____

_____

_____

_____

_____

_____

_____

_____

_____

_____

_____

_____

_____

_____

Do not forget to film a video!

CHILDHOOD

Standing at the edge of an open space alone and forgotten about with nothing in front of him but invisible oxygen that was hard to breathe. Thoughts were racing through his mind that forged imprints within his soul he would never forget; no child should ever have these thoughts. Memory is the blessing of survival, but simultaneously the curse to living. The weight of his world wore down on him daily as the island he owned was his land of social existence persuading others against making his acquaintance. He was an outlier. He was misunderstood, unloved, unwanted, and unstoppable in his self-hatred. As he stood there alone in the same spot, the same bell rang each day and conditioned him to feel suicidal, self-ashamed and resentful. The idea of a better life never crossed his mind; therefore, he had to use his imagination. Creativity became his zone of existence and the only reason according to him to be. Creativity was his muse as he was so alone that he became ashamed to be present around his peers even when they would reach out in peace, love and friendship…it was all invisible to his eye. The language of love was unbeknownst to him and there was no hope. One may ask who this could be. He is your writer, he is me. This hell was my childhood. I was only twelve.

Memory is the blessing of survival, but simultaneously the curse to living. - Childhood

_____

_____

_____

_____

_____

_____

_____

_____

_____

_____

_____

_____

_____

_____

_____

_____

_____

Do not forget to film a video!

Refer to page i for directions

Keep reading!
Keep writing!
Keep Filming!

DON'T FORGET TO FILM YOUR VIDEO!

Tag us when you're done!
 Culture Matters
 cultureunitesauthors

#thirtydaysofthought
#culturematters
#readwritespeak
#cultureunitesauthors

Exponential Growth

The dividend with an unequaled return on investment is growth. Most would never think to try, and few will seek out and find. Our hidden garden is our potential, and as we water it every day expecting a result, we only create disappointment over ourselves. Our personal growth takes a lot of time, our whole entire life, as we are always growing.

Just as we want to give up and quit, we must view ourselves and what we are fighting for. The treasures of our heart lie in wisdom. A seed of hope and understanding waits to blossom until the Spring. Growth itself is not a linear process, it may not happen today, and it may not happen tomorrow, but all great fears are worth striving for.

A leader who is willing to persist through adversity will mount his fate and come out the other side of growth. But now the leader encompasses growth. The leader has a purpose and his growth is exponential.

"Growth itself is not a linear process, it may not happen today, and it may not happen tomorrow, but all great fears are worth striving for." – Exponential Growth

_____

_____

_____

_____

_____

_____

_____

_____

_____

_____

_____

_____

_____

_____

_____

_____

Do not forget to film a video!

CULTURE OF PRIDE

If happiness and fear are gone, no ill emotion may harm us. Not apathy, grief, guilt or even anger. None can do us harm but of our own self-infatuation and pride. As the lion stalks its prey, the lion has only one focus and one sole reason to breathe. The King of King's only truth is his rank on the biological pedestal. He is King of the jungle, and head of his pride. He is self-centered, and it is as abundant as the blade of a razor, like hairs from his chin to helm. He is but a creature being his best self, a true killing machine built strong yet unknown to any other future. For this King of Kings has no other pride, the King of all living- not the toughest nor the quickest, but the most social. Quick to self-sacrifice for the greater good, this King of all great Kings has no ceiling or boundaries of love, peace and joy known to him. Only due to one's choice, can this King of all Kings claim his eternal truth. That with every single decision he makes reboots his own self truth.

God unveils himself if only for a moment, between the instinct of pride and the decision of courage. This King of all Kings is man. You know him well. You are him. Choose to step out of your own shadow, King, be courageous. Be oh great. King of all Kings, master of all living. BE MAN.

"If happiness and fear are gone, no ill emotion may harm us." – Culture of Pride

_____

_____

_____

_____

_____

_____

_____

_____

_____

_____

_____

_____

_____

Do not forget to film a video!

WRITE IT DOWN

Without it written down, it may be lost forever. Our truth we hold unto ourselves along with our inner demons and outer callings; they beckon to be set free and able to roam the earth we all share. The thoughts we cycle throughout the canyons of our mind scream loudly and clearly our message of truth or call to reason. We own our truths, but if we do not write them down, they will be lost. It is our duty and our right to make our truths resonate with our fellow men. The obligation is presented at our birth to share and only we may decide upon this action and it begins by writing it down. Upon transcription our soul quivers, and every essence of our being gasps with reluctance and exhales in relief. It is in our human nature to hold the demons inside. We hold on for dear life because the fear of failure and rejection protects us from finding out our true potentials fate. Would our brethren be in awe or sigh with disgrace? What could be our outcome if the latter held true? These false evidences appear as real as the pen we hold through our thought creations, and as the pens ink fades into our parchment we realize our fate was made prior to our beginning. As we all arrive at the same destination in the first place it must become our duty to prevent our questions from being unanswered. It will only plague us. What if I were heard? Who may I have touched? Am I accepted? At our life's moment last breath all we wanted was always so clear, and we will be content if we write.

We own our truths, but if we do not write them down, they will be lost. – Write It Down

_____

_____

_____

_____

_____

_____

_____

_____

_____

_____

_____

_____

_____

_____

_____

_____

Do not forget to film a video!

Refer to page i for directions

Keep reading!
Keep writing!
Keep Filming!

DON'T FORGET TO FILM YOUR VIDEO!

Tag us when you're done!
f Culture Matters
⊙ cultureunitesauthors

#thirtydaysofthought
#culturematters
#readwritespeak
#cultureunitesauthors

APPROACHABLE

Talk. Don't be afraid to speak to a stranger because everyone has a story to be heard. As sayings go, this one holds the weight of the worlds. The sheer mass of life experiences intertwined in heaped conversation and expansive volume creates opportunity. When we let our guards down to essentially open ourselves up, anything is possible from there, so pass go, collect $200 and start your journey. Lean into discomfort. Life has officially started, and you are authentic and approachable. Life has a fickle way of twisting and turning, and we never are quite sure how we fit in each other's movie but be it for only the debut or a lead role, this journey we are on is together. Biology holds truth over us that we are meant to connect. We are supposed to rely on each other because then we create an observer and observed relationship. We get real with ourselves and each other and we find truths we never deemed possible. We find a certain truth in approachability that becomes a necessity in the meaning of purpose. After all, if we can survive cooperating with one another, learning from each other's actions and reactions, and common contribution of innate mechanisms of fulfillment then that trail needs to begin with being approachable. No ship has ever sailed, no cathedral ever built, and no family has been fostered without someone or some task being approachable. Find it within, learn it and create it. Talk! Don't be afraid to talk to strangers. Be approachable.

"The sheer mass of life experiences intertwined in heaped conversation and expansive volume creates opportunity." – Approachable

_____

_____

_____

_____

_____

_____

_____

_____

_____

_____

_____

_____

_____

_____

Do not forget to film a video!

RELATIONSHIPS

What are relationships? After one thousand years our common definition may still be unclear. Considering turnover in businesses, the current divorce rate and who we all personally stay friends with throughout our entire life, it's hard to know what relationships are. Let's say for arguments sake that relationships are understanding. Now, let's go even further and say relationships are the transference of energy and the alignment of beliefs that translate into common actions. Therefore, transference of thought energy and the acceptance of belief lead to mutually beneficial actions that strengthen the mind, heart and spirit of all parties involved in the relationship. This is love. Would that make relationships love? Write your thoughts down. Speak your truth and cause the earth to rotate faster with your creativity. Our mutual understanding is a relationship worth fighting for. It is a human one.

Relationships are understanding. – Relationships

_____

_____

_____

_____

_____

_____

_____

_____

_____

_____

_____

_____

_____

_____

_____

Do not forget to film a video!

ACCEPTING DIFFERENT SOCKS

"To each their own," I dare to say with fiery conviction! We are but matches in the same pack and stuck together creating a flame. We seek purpose from an outside source to realize the core ingredients of our nature within us the entire time. Our uses are abundant no matter how we appear and considering our genetic comparison we each have brilliance within us. While obtaining the understanding of our self-core and acceptance of our unique qualities as a unit make us whole. I call this perception, "Accepting Different Socks." Are you accepting each for their own or misunderstanding the beauty in our differences? We all know what it is like to sit down comfortably and mild mannered at the nearby coffee shop ready to work, when all the sudden perplexity reveals its foul head. Our perplexity emanates from the inquisitive, irritable, confused, confounded, indifferent or upset thoughts combusting simultaneously from an odd sight of the nearby stranger wearing two different socks. All our conversations contain right or wrong morals or ethics congealed with negative and child-like reptile actions that stream into our minds. We are reminded of childhood, our parents, our schooling or lack thereof, and social norms drowned upon us since the ripe old age of forever, and we become convicted by our cause. Unbeknownst to us this is the level of unknown that has been unconsciously factored in this emotive justification to pry and dive into another's life. Our flame burns bright with self-righteous dogma where we feel compelled to ignite 'the chase' in yet another victim. The idea of individualization runs dry in context to who we are, what we believe and how we instinctively respond. Different socks for different folks are not the norm, but abnormal that we tend to hate with fear, anger and the desire to change. Our flame is unknown to us that the entire match box we have may all burn out igniting every flame while devastating all those around us causing unchangeable catastrophe. This is all due to the following misperception of another's different socks. Our sense of possession over what socks are the right pair, and proper to wear. All in all, is there one true answer? No never. How can there ever be? Unless we are told what to do, we must decide and our decision without guidance comes as subjective. This subjectivity we cannot control, but we can recognize our individuality of the flame we all share yet differ in, as well as the beauty of our different socks whether we decide to wear them or not. When in doubt, decide to accept different socks as your world may end up being a better place. Right now, look down. What color socks are you wearing? And your neighbor?

Our uses are abundant no matter how we appear and considering our genetic comparison we each have brilliance within us. – Accepting Different Socks

_____

_____

_____

_____

_____

_____

_____

_____

_____

_____

_____

_____

_____

_____

_____

_____

Do not forget to film a video!

Refer to page i for directions

Keep reading!
Keep writing!
Keep Filming!

DON'T FORGET TO FILM YOUR VIDEO!

Tag us when you're done!
⬛ Culture Matters
⬛ cultureunitesauthors

#thirtydaysofthought
#culturematters
#readwritespeak
#cultureunitesauthors

GETTING STUCK

Lost in transition and stuck in first gear when the mechanisms work but the operators don't. How often have we been perfect for the job, yet stuck in the gears of life? We feel jammed in what is possible and what is facing us. The figment of our imagination so close to manifestation is just at that tip of the pen, but so far as the words just do not ring true. The words are but useless dribble jotted on the page or consisting of philosophical rants perpetuated over run-on sentences. The woes of creativity reign true the longer we continue to labor solutions to problems. Sometimes the only way to save face is to just show up. Pen in hand, head on straight, heart in tune to the beat of its drum and the writer with a sound message. Life, writing, winning, and humanity all the same are about getting unstuck. Persevere in due course; your message is commitment and solidarity. No matter our cluttered conscience or our blocked vision for the day we show up ready and able as the day's confidence kicks back in. We remind ourselves this is who we are. We are only human, and the best writers will still get stuck.

Life, writing, winning, and humanity all the same are about getting unstuck. Persevere in due course; your message is commitment and solidarity. – Getting Stuck

_____

_____

_____

_____

_____

_____

_____

_____

_____

_____

_____

_____

_____

_____

_____

Do not forget to film a video!

I Quit, Every Day
I'm the Entrepreneur

I am thinking of an assembly line, white backdrop with black spots stick out in mind and the fear of the unknown but not quite a sense of what is. These creatures slowly creeping to their maker is that of the entrepreneurial climb. It's 10 A.M. and the alarm has gone off seven times, 4:55 A.M.-click off, 5:25 A.M. -click off, 5:45, 6:05, 6:45, 8:30, 9 A.M. - click, click, click off! The decision has been made, and I'm mad now, but I'm no cow, I am an entrepreneur, and an angry one at that. I am in my own way and cannot get out of it. The only thing reasonable that comes to mind starts and ends with a four-letter word, quit. Come to think of it, quotes got me here remembering of the cute success stories they like to sponsor on Facebook, "Entrepreneurship is like eating glass" – Elon Musk. Today I know the feeling; every day is the same glass and the tried and true method of eating it. The job is to have no fear my role is to fight the fire. The sole responsibility of me, the CEO, is to do the dirty work- to man my own conveyer belt and feed my people with this mad meat. They will never know the truth, the hell, they cannot see inside the factory of bullshit. The omissions I hold back, they cannot see the cleanliness, the tears, the screams, the pain inside, and I hold the burden. Every night the same dream of white body and black spots, fear in their eyes as the curtailers leading the herd of "yes men" near their destination. They feed their people, the unclear unknowing people following the master controller, the mad cow himself. I lay here 10 A.M., clock ticking louder, redundant, revered, yet resented by myself, my people and my cows. I must decide, and it must be to face the day. What other choice do I have? Only one, "Good morning Facebook! I love Monday, (meme face), (happy sticker), (exclamation, exclamation), whooo!! Who else loves their work?" This is the entrepreneur, and still, I want to eat the grass of my cows?

"I must decide, and it must be to face the day." – I Quit, Every Day I'm The Entrepreneur

_____

_____

_____

_____

_____

_____

_____

_____

_____

_____

_____

_____

_____

_____

Do not forget to film a video!

Writer's Block

A mental dam meant to break. Unlike the purest of liquids, water holds itself safe for our keeping and the utility of consumption. A mind full of thoughts unable to flow out becomes toxic quickly. You see, the mind can be a very dark place when everyone is home. All your ideals, fears, hopes and dreams refusing to let themselves out on your paper but cooped up inside your cortex arguing for your attention. Focus is impossible, stress is indefinite, and anxiety is seemingly the only outcome. When there is a dam in your mind holding back your genius, you have awakened through self-exploration and no new life may be born from the ideas festering within you. This is the anti-spiritual, non-organic, biologically unacceptable and psychologically misaligning; the catalyst to your next genius exploration; the storm to your rainbow. There are no positive outcomes if thoughts stay caged and are unable to flow, therefore, do not give up nor give in. The mental dam you may be absorbing serves a purpose. This may come to you as a light warning that if you break your "Culture Oath" to read, write and speak every day this may happen to you too. When culture is not upheld, and your thoughts remain in your mind for too long, you may find yourself feeling down, and sometimes even a little crazy. This is writer's block. Stay true to your heart and be persistent with your mind. Your mind will only love you more for it, and that is beautiful, that is creation.

"You see, the mind can be a very dark place when everyone is home."
– Writer's Block

_____

_____

_____

_____

_____

_____

_____

_____

_____

_____

_____

_____

_____

_____

_____

_____

Do not forget to film a video!

Refer to page i for directions

Keep reading!
Keep writing!
Keep Filming!

DON'T FORGET TO FILM YOUR VIDEO!

Tag us when you're done!
 Culture Matters
 cultureunitesauthors

#thirtydaysofthought
#culturematters
#readwritespeak
#cultureunitesauthors

Seven Days A Week

Picture a vat of butter. Its composite is creamy and textured, smooth and thick. It represents our lives full of richness, experiences and memories of pleasure that bring us back to better times, but wisdom hindering our souls for the coming future. The future we create. As the butter continues to churn, time continues to pass by. Days go by without a muse. When our head stays down focused on our given task, our purpose has been handed down and bestowed upon us by destiny. A purpose forged from a greater vision, and of a better life. As the days go by, we forget who we knew, we distract ourselves from the fear of thought while the pain inside stays numb for just a little while longer. The vat of butter- our life is swirled into its grandest potential or its deepest oblivion. The question is motion. How are we stirring our vat? How are we stirring up our lives and those we touch through the journey? These seven days will pass regardless, but how will we use them? In all this time we may not ask these vital questions when all we must spend is seven days. The answers to these questions are monumental. At deaths inevitable door most will meet the same foe; regret. We will ask ourselves why, what and how come we didn't try? If only we knew the importance of these seven days. We can imagine our vat. Our vat is our resource of potential and it is stirred in congruence with our actions. Unfortunately, due to ignorance, its taste may be foul, but all we can say in our last possible breath will be, "I can't believe it's not butter." The truth remains, your butter might not be my butter, but if it fits your criteria of butter you asked the correct questions, you met the expectations, and you took the actions to complete your task. You applied potent knowledge in your seven days, and for that we can turn to those we meet and say it mattered. Our truth created our future.

"When our head stays down on our given task, our purpose had been handed down and bestowed upon us by destiny." – Seven Days A Week

_____

_____

_____

_____

_____

_____

_____

_____

_____

_____

_____

_____

_____

_____

_____

_____

Do not forget to film a video!

Domino Effect

Everything has a start, but its end we may never know. Unfathomable to our mind is what has slightly passed cognition; pure potentiality. Imagination is one grand domino effect and the beginning of all things' great starts with a singular blast of thought. This rocket ship or idea can travel to any destination in the universe, known or unknown to man. One doubling after the other leads to unquantifiable outcomes, and some not even the brightest among us may comprehend. A certain dictum of faith will be paramount in adhering to the actions necessary to execute in this imagined reality. This is, The Domino Effect, and as powerful as its outcome to the naked eye may appear, we may still need faith. The conviction behind the belief thrusts upon the idea that resulted from the initial thought. The thought intertwined in a puzzle of perception that makes up the life we happen to bring meaning to what we know and conceive. Simply, we are all products of the eternal domino effect of the universe which is full of potentialities, unlimited learning, earning, and yearning potentials. These potentials are pragmatically executed upon those who know this truth. However, the lie is The Domino Effect.

Imagination is one grand domino effect and the beginning of all thing's great starts with a singular blast of thought. – Domino Effect

_____

_____

_____

_____

_____

_____

_____

_____

_____

_____

_____

_____

_____

_____

_____

_____

Do not forget to film a video!

EXHAUSTION 101

My eyelids grow heavy and my pen drifts slowly. Each motion weighs heavy as if I am not mentally prepared for my usual routine to pour out my heart and convey my powerful message of wisdom and of power. My hand starts to quiver as each moment passes and my usual tone will get lost in the masses. It seems I am so exhausted, that I am even starting to rhyme.

Shut down mode... You must get rest; you must reboot your brain. I believe that from the moment I was born it has been instilled in me that without mental fortitude all days of life would be taken. When it comes to exhaustion, that thought can be skewed, and we cannot have that. We cannot ever deliver an unclear message. It is not fair to us and it is not fair to our audience. However, commitment mixed with exhaustion is a strange and funny thing. Although exhaustion has set in and honest frustration has compounded, I have committed to writing, and I will be completely uniting. I am tying together this script and these scripts of what I believe is the deliverable message for you, my readers, to help, coach, teach, and explain that projects must get completed. Sleep must not be taken for granted. Do not allow exhaustion to become an uncompleted mission, because those missions are going to change lives. Until next time, goodnight.

Do not allow exhaustion to become an uncompleted mission, because those missions are going to change lives. – Exhaustion 101

_____

_____

_____

_____

_____

_____

_____

_____

_____

_____

_____

_____

_____

_____

Do not forget to film a video!

Refer to page i for directions

Keep reading!
Keep writing!
Keep Filming!

DON'T FORGET TO FILM YOUR VIDEO!

Tag us when you're done!
Culture Matters
cultureunitesauthors

#thirtydaysofthought
#culturematters
#readwritespeak
#cultureunitesauthors

Culture Shock

After all that has been digested one could dizzily fall off their socially constructed pedestal, recognize the dog that chases them, their ego, and come to a new understanding of self. They just might bring true value to themselves and others yet take away material wealth, social status, and self-appointed credo of importance, and what could they have left? The answer is nothing, and everything. In your nakedness you have mind, body and spirit; the power to make changes. Change within you is first, and then change within others is guaranteed. You, the reader, are a special, beautiful human gift to the world. Genius lies within you, and this book is meant to uncover it. This tool you have uncovered, dug through, read, absorbed, contemplated over, argued with, chastised, and cried amongst is meant to enable your craftsmanship to forge a better you. For the truest you to let go and walk into the light as simple efforts must be made. Yes, this is a culture shock, but for the utility of this text to make an impact forever you must take ownership. Read every morning, read every afternoon, and read every evening. Do this for ten minutes each day, along with speaking, and diligently transcribe your arguments with this text on the other page. Every day, film a video of what you read, thought, or wrote or all the above. If you do this daily, you will grow. Use this writing and speaking time to grapple with yourself, clear your head, and whisk away the smog of doubt along with the fear and trembling with whatever ill thoughts plague your mind. Clean out the cobwebs of your skull and let your wisdom that has been caged up inside your head free. Allow your wisdom to fly daily with social media and film one minute of deliberate vocal expression of what you wrote. The layers of skin of who you were will shed themselves and the being who you could not comprehend inside will be unleashed. This is the new you, this is the confident, revelatory, articulate, radiant, forthright, truthful, courageous, loving, accepting, thoughtful, blissful, and peaceful you. This reader, this writer, and this speaker is YOU! You are your own hero, and we are here to guide you, inspire you, and prep you for battle. The war with your worst self will now be defeated, and the dark will juxtapose the light inside and your genius will shine forth. For within your dark places lies a giant sun ready to make its debut. Continue, reading, writing and speaking with 30 Days of Thought. Continue to be courageous and share what you read, write and speak. This is a culture shock- we support your growth. You are something. You are genius. You are light.

PROCRASTINATION IS THE ONLY TRUE DEATH

To put off or to let go, or simply wait for an opportunity means death. For what exactly could we possibly need to get started? It will never be what we have but only what we believe we need that will stop us. The potential of what is may just be the effect of the cause; the action itself and not the fears that stalk our mind. When we perceive our only true death as the lack of execution upon a thought our paradigm will never be the same. The understanding of our power and the essence of life itself may be realized in the distinction between thinking and getting started. As the adage goes, "procrastination is the art of living in our yesterday, avoiding today and destroying tomorrow." -Ben Franklin

To live in doing the same thing repeatedly expecting a different result is the definition of insanity. If you have already lived that truth once, why entertain living it a second time? The life of now lies in the execution of energy exerted in thinking, speaking, and writing. The fruits of our labor are the manifestation of tomorrow. Procrastination or the act of putting things off is surely the only true death. If this truth holds its weight that knowing is the bridge between the negative and the positive or the source be it physical or non-physical then the only true death is to never begin. Our biggest fear is death, but an imagined reality of what may be coming next only to prove that there is something next shows that we are not ready for death at all. Be true to this statement as procrastination is but a feeling from the past. Procrastination does not exist, but only in your mind and avoiding creation is guaranteeing one probable future, failure in not starting. Make your choice wisely.

The potential of what is may just be the effect of the cause; the action itself. – Procrastination is the Only True Death

_____

_____

_____

_____

_____

_____

_____

_____

_____

_____

_____

_____

_____

_____

_____

Do not forget to film a video!

CAN'T READ MINDS

To assume is to make an ass out of you and me. The awareness of this perception suggests that I cannot read minds. All I have is my truth and the trust I may ascertain from others in times of quiet contemplation. I'm lying on my back staring blankly into space with your face staring back at mine. The times we had and days we lost due to miscommunication plague me like something foul. It is moments like this when reflection and harsh contemplation remind me of why you'd say, "don't assume, it only makes an ass out of you and me." I'm reminded of the times I spoke and didn't intend to listen. The arguments founded on my ignorance and lack of empathy for all those times, I'm here to tell you, I'm sorry. Sorry could never be enough but it must still be said in turn for my behavior. I want to dive deep into a new course of action that of listening to ask questions leads to all the answers from within. After my mistakes, I have taken ownership and invested in self-knowledge of what must be. What must be is to listen for I cannot read minds. Living life loosely and speeding to every next level caught me up in the throes of narcissisms by being present or listening whilst in the "stew." The "stew" is defined as a melting pot of self-absorption, vanity, intoxication and self-importance. Without realizing my wrongs, I pulled you and everyone into my vortex of selfishness and only now do I realize I can't read minds. The hurt I cast on you, your friends and those around us makes me feel uncomfortable but I must realize my woes if they are ever to not be in vain. From this I can and will learn to be a better man and with that I promise you that I know now and forever, I can't read minds...

"I want to dive deep into a new course of action that of listening to ask questions leads all the answers from within." – Can't Read Minds

_____

_____

_____

_____

_____

_____

_____

_____

_____

_____

_____

_____

_____

_____

_____

_____

_____

Do not forget to film a video!

Refer to page i for directions

Keep reading!
Keep writing!
Keep Filming!

DON'T FORGET TO FILM YOUR VIDEO!

Tag us when you're done!
 Culture Matters
 cultureunitesauthors

#thirtydaysofthought
#culturematters
#readwritespeak
#cultureunitesauthors

No Such Thing
as a Millennial

There is no such thing as a millennial. To be born in a specific time is as irrelevant as any word dedicated to whatever meaning is chosen for it. The label always limits when the meaning is misunderstood. Whenever we cover up any topic with a label rooted in unintelligible philosophies that haven't been properly dissected, we cannot help but to cause chaos. We, the millennials are chaos. Due to this ignorance, our human condition is under the influence of limitation through our thoughtfulness and our fates being sealed by said limitations of our own words. There is no such thing as, we, the millennial!!! They call us young, uncaring, undisciplined, unequal, misguided, misaligned, deliberately desperate and unconsciously enslaved by devices. The common tongue throws daggers at our motivation and fills our balloons of creativity with hatred that the masses believe will pop as they are heightened. Our apparent lack of work ethos is commonly uncommon in the past societies we have been born, yet we sit back in silence waiting for proof that there is in fact hope for our future. All fingers point to the millennial in a negative connotation in respect to our character. I say finger point away! The minds of our predecessors are full of condemnation and resentment, they resent us for who we are appearing *not* to be and condemn us for a world we are living in that they created. Nothing we do is enough, and whatever we speak of doing next is inevitably shut down. Our words are weak, the hearts we show have no blood flow and to those who pass judgment we are viewed as zombies feeding off one corpse. America, a land we have inherited, left unto us from our forefathers, our current state of empowerment we are in with racism, bigotry, hate, and false platitudes we have been born into are not of our doing. They are of our makers, and we are just able to have the means to "give in," and not for what we need or want, but for what humans do. They are wrong about us. We are not limited by our fixations on anything. Our conscious is real, raw, and true to all things human. We are not millennials, we are humans. We are but free to think, to feel and to be present. We are love, we are compassion, and we are empathy. We are connected, and our global movement is that of one. We are caught up with the common norms: fear, love, self-righteousness, but we will get through that and not allow the belittling and limiting with labels. We are tired, we are drained and without hesitations in our claim, we are not millennials. We are human, and we are now. We will not sit down; we will not shut up and we will not give up. We will be heard. There is no such thing as a millennial.

"The label always limits when the meaning is misunderstood." – No Such Thing as a Millennial

_____

_____

_____

_____

_____

_____

_____

_____

_____

_____

_____

_____

_____

_____

_____

_____

_____

Do not forget to film a video!

SPEAK

It all starts from your gut. This immense power festers from within, and as your body begins to decompress this somewhat squeamish yet necessary feeling arises. What feels like fire begins to bubble up inside waiting for the oratory to begin, and as time passes the moments just before you speak stand still. The crowd stares back waiting to be pleased caring for their own salvation and you think to yourself "Is this what it means to be a speaker?" You pause, reflect and then continue onward unaffected. There is a calming feeling that comes over you with an understanding you will do well, and that this is in fact your purpose. You will open the minds in your audience and put the beats back in their hearts fulfilling everything you stand for. Your speech will make others feel more aware than the minute before you started and the dead silence before and during feels like your truth is becoming one with your audience. The truth lives on in your word. If only the act itself was easy; a task of the courageous with every voice inside your head muffled, yet your story clearer than ever. You have practiced, and you have done your due diligence for your message to be clear, and regardless of your timing it will be clear. The words you choose along with the words you feel will spread through the minds of those who you are forming an agreement with for the first time. You will save a lot of souls because of your courage to learn, think, grow and share. Your idea- raw and pure is a revelation to the masses. Your spark of power comes from within and gives you the personal power to share. Your audience becomes your creation, and in this truth, you have decided to voice your will to live forever. If God is creation and decision leads to creation then your voice has brought you as close to God as we may ever be in our existence, and all due to your choice. The choice you chose to speak.

"Your speech will make others feel more aware than the minute before you started and the dead silence before and during feels like your truth is becoming one with your audience." – Speak

_____

_____

_____

_____

_____

_____

_____

_____

_____

_____

_____

_____

_____

_____

_____

_____

_____

_____

Do not forget to film a video!

INFORMATION AGE

Throughout history one thing has always come to change; culture. When Alexander, the son of Zeus conquered the known world at the age of 31, his influence is all of what lasted. It may not have been Alexander the Greats' heir who reaped the benefits of his savage grind but those who conquered, the survivors and the cultured witnessed the coming information age. History tells no lies but only happenstance and circumstance therefore, due to Alexander's conquests, the eastern world benefitted from the desert to the forest timberlands of Mother Russia up in India into Egypt itself. The common tongue left the possibility of a new religion to spread 300+ years later, Christianity. All of this due to one man and *that* is the power of culture.

Throughout time, there have been times of great progress and of enormous dread. Through the spread of ignorance, malevolence, fear, and even hope a ruler is needed.

Today is a new day; it is your world to conquer. In this new age of information, of hope and of light anything is possible. Without fear of persecution or extreme harm we may all soak in the knowledge and bask in the euphoria of knowing we may bear influence. Like the western world post printing press or the Egyptian empire at height for the first time, us common folk may absorb, purify and spread information. For the first time, the power leans towards the masses and it is our cultures' responsibility to spread positivity and joy. We must submit to this responsibility. The world has changed, and we must adapt because without adapting our empire will crumble, we will perish, and our culture will die. Similarly, to the trials of past generations we will get overthrown and absorbed by a stronger foe; a better enemy. A competitor ready and aware, in the days of information- knowledge is power to be reined in with action and foresight. It is our duty in this time to be aware because information matters and our conquerors have proven that. Let's raise our swords and make a vow forever to be aware of the information that is provided to us. Spread the word, and commit to our current culture, because culture matters.

"Today is a new day; it is your world to conquer." – Information Age

_____

_____

_____

_____

_____

_____

_____

_____

_____

_____

_____

_____

_____

_____

_____

_____

Do not forget to film a video!

Refer to page i for directions

Keep reading!
Keep writing!
Keep Filming!

DON'T FORGET TO FILM YOUR VIDEO!

Tag us when you're done!
 Culture Matters
 cultureunitesauthors

#thirtydaysofthought
#culturematters
#readwritespeak
#cultureunitesauthors

HUMANS SHOULDN'T BE COPS

The year is 2040 and humans shouldn't be cops. The brave one stands perched in a position of power, his hands brace the podium, his grip tight and his knuckles white with vigor. He possesses feelings of anger, pain and passion that courses through his veins. He speaks the word of a nation and says what the mass is thinking but cannot speak. He says, "rise up, raise your level of being, be open, be curious, be patient, be genuine, be loving, be good and just, rise up my brethren, but take a knee to enforcement!" Calmness washes over the mass like a newborn cleansed by their mother in their first bath, all sins become absolved. The citizens listen intently to understand and not to reply, however something is not all there. The common communication takes place: the act of justifying jobs, positions and engagements which if we are rising, we should be increasing our societal being, but it does not appear that way. Therefore, we must take aim at one of the forefathers of antiquated valor; this symbol is that of law enforcement. I dare say what all must hear humans should not be cops. Policing, beating, enforcement of proper conduct, prosecution of peace, for we the people should be able to explore and be free, but the reasons above prevent that based on a human's interpretation of law enforcement. This is what keeps the cycle of hell juxtaposed to an ideal we call democracy. If we are to grow to evolve and dissolve the chains of primal man we must rally to a cause and rise as our keepers' voices. We must fight a new and greater fight, that of the educated human. We must outsource our muscle to the non-organic and take heed of the coming signs of evolution. It is better for us to decide to love artificial intelligence because humans should not be cops– that's what robots are for. Any role, responsibility or creed disempowering another man lowers that of the other man, the enforcer with fire in his eyes. A cycle of human disempowerment and a shackling of growth- humans will not evolve this way. The abyss becomes a terrible and scary pattern. This pattern is one of force, hell, pride, and control, and the longer we stare into the abyss, the more likely it is to stare back at us eventually owning us as it has up to this point. We can prevent playing with this kind of fire, and we can start by not allowing humans to be cops. Call it blasphemous, cry for my persecution, and for the straight jacket of silence to befall this outcry, and do so in vain because regardless of culture, technology heals all wounds be it benign or malignant. I foreshadow this job of policemen and policewomen being replaced by artificial intelligence. If we want to evolve in finally being humans, humans should not be cops.

Dedicated to those brave enough to enforce common law in a world not wise enough yet to be at peace. Thank you for your service.

"If we are to grow to evolve and dissolve the chains of primal man we must rally to a cause and rise as our keeper voices. We must fight a new and greater fight, that of the educated human. We must outsource our muscle to the non-organic and take heed of the coming signs of evolution. It is better for us to decide to love artificial intelligence because humans should not be cops." – Humans Shouldn't Be Cops

_____

_____

_____

_____

_____

_____

_____

_____

_____

_____

_____

_____

_____

_____

_____

_____

_____

Do not forget to film a video!

FREAKED OUT

Freaked out and bewildered by the truth that not everything is going to be okay. The false sense of security can be a silent killer. We can kid ourselves too often by thinking everything will just turn out okay. Usually this mantra is not the case. Often, we need to go through a near death experience to shatter our mental paradigm and rattle the cage of mediocrity we have been stuck in. Usually without realizing it, our self-defeating habits weigh heavily on ourselves like a 500-lb. gorilla sitting on our chests preventing normal breathing. SO, WAKE UP!

When forced under pressure, most are not ready and willing to glimmer with hope of what could be instead of understanding glimmer in its entirety with not hope, but confidence. We put forth the effort of what, "should be" and to be perfect in moments of pressure we in turn find our true selves. To believe in one's self, to exude confidence and ooze with passion is our only real mirror of belief. We measure the mass of our belief in ourselves by the dream we see and the vision we turn it into. Are you one to dig deep? Will you take a deep breath and follow through- or will you just freak out…?

"The false sense of security can be a silent killer." – Freaked Out

_____

_____

_____

_____

_____

_____

_____

_____

_____

_____

_____

_____

_____

_____

_____

_____

_____

Do not forget to film a video!

INFORMATION OVERLOAD

At light speed every possible orifice of our being is bombarded by emotion. It can be positive or negative; it can be lusting or loving like a pendulum swinging our fate and fulfillment held in the grip of consumption. The need to earn, a drive to show capital gain or promise to stand tall amongst our peers, these animalistic tendencies holds us hostage to our worst selves. The reptilian ego hides inside its barred layer just waiting to be unleashed. Our hands tightly gripped to the bars of its domain like a prison made of pure information with our culture identified clearly that we live in fear. We wait patiently for the next update, holding onto a hope of a better tomorrow. In an era of information overload, and a culture of conformity we have lost our identity and we have succumbed to thoughts we feel we need. We have gained a never-ending hunger for falsehood and it classifies itself something that can never be enough, and we can potentially look back in horror, at the demons, at the reptile, at ourselves.

What we see now are not just falsehoods but the ugly truths. The age of information overload shows us losing sight of who we are, what matters and a culture of brotherhood and compassion we had. In an overloaded day the "I" matters- the selfish manifestation of consumerism will always rain true in the eye of the beholder. This culture staring deeply into its own reflection is only able to perceive what it has been cultivated for good or evil. As we stay on our path for "self" it is always hard to see the whole production when we are just a small fragment even though our role is so important. Two words may come to some of us as we drift away- do you dare to speak them to become aware? Be wary of your reflection as it will not hesitate to show your truth.

"Be wary of your reflection as it will not hesitate to show your truth."
– Information Overload

_____

_____

_____

_____

_____

_____

_____

_____

_____

_____

_____

_____

_____

_____

Do not forget to film a video!

Refer to page i for directions

Keep reading!
Keep writing!
Keep Filming!

DON'T FORGET TO FILM YOUR VIDEO!

Tag us when you're done!
Culture Matters
cultureunitesauthors

#thirtydaysofthought
#culturematters
#readwritespeak
#cultureunitesauthors

INTELLECTUAL PASSION
DRIVES OUT SENSUALITY

Blazing hot be it a yearning for maternal affection, material possession or a reptilian-mammalian emotive self-protection, the human
pulls the strings to the lost puppet, his false self, and the actor he
shows the world. Without aim he conjures up fruitless thoughts of
yearning self-effacing acts and hedonistic desires that play out in his
day to day. Our puppet is caged by the fog of ignorance and enslaved
by the unconscious habituation of unknowing. By happenstance
may he break free, not by his genetic predisposition or by the will
of his predecessor or mentor will he manifest the charms of intel-
lect or curiosity, but purely through accidental environmental woes.
He will bet on the luck of the draw. His cognitive pull does not
come through him but aims to him through life's uncanny chances
of probability. He is the chosen one in this case. The puppet with
scissors for his string, the curiosity to break free, the intelligence to
forbear against what comes natural- sensuality. The urges are ever
present, but the interest is a mask. The weight that holds down his
demon, wings clipped, and pestilence contained. Our puppet is held
to fervent ideas that of imagination and discovery. To have both curiosity and sensuality is in vogue. The forsaken genius distracted by
talent and insecurity is a sacrifice that must be made, and the choice
is an easy one.

"His cognitive pull does not come through him but aims to him through life's uncanny chances of probability." – Intellectual Passion Drives Out Sensuality

_____

_____

_____

_____

_____

_____

_____

_____

_____

_____

_____

_____

_____

_____

_____

Do not forget to film a video!

DARK COMPANION

From pain comes purpose and in that seed of hope your dark companion is born, conflict. Birthed in pitch black and dreary contempt through self-pity our phoenix inside glazed with fiery passion waits to be awakened. There are times in our lives where fate knocks, but nobody is home, or even worse doubt creeps in our back door blocking our footsteps to freedom. Every dream we have dreamed mixed with all our hopes are merely on the other side and all we must do is turn the knob to pull ourselves to salvation. Often, we get lost in our own devices and without realizing it our pain dominates our passion. I know this story too well due to my history with pain. Born rejected and thought to be an unlovable orphan, the offspring of an unfit addict with no rhyme or reason to love a child. My plight in life started at the top of a police officer's desk only three months after my birth. Life for me started in pain, but luckily for me, and my now future audiences this adversity has turned my pain into my purpose to tell a story, a story that can help others. It was the seeing on the other side of a bleak outcome and a vision of a better tomorrow. This story gave me a better alternative and created a purpose for me; how my pain has become my purpose. My dark companion burns bright and he smiles today upon our future.

Dedicated to The Liar Lid Book

Every dream we have dreamed mixed with all our hopes are merely on the other side and all we must do is turn the knob to pull ourselves to salvation. – Dark Companion

_____

_____

_____

_____

_____

_____

_____

_____

_____

_____

_____

_____

_____

_____

_____

Do not forget to film a video!

CULTURE CREATES MATTER

The premise to Culture Matters is weighed on Newton himself. The physical laws we have come to understand are the framework to the belief that culture does matter. It was in fact, Einstein who said that energy and matter is the same thing, but in different form. The reality of our nature itself may be open for subjective discussion, but our objective view is that between Newton and Einstein, physics and science- culture does in fact create matter. The subjective equals the objective which is the imagistic to materialistic.

We all share the miniature satellites each of us has been bestowed upon by our maker himself. This ability for the influencer to believe, then see in the mind. The ability to help others see to believe shows us culture matters. It is belief in the imagined, the invisible and non-physical that causes the marriage of thoughts and action to determine any outcome.

These outcomes are the visible and physical manifestations of energy and thoughts figurative in nature. The reality we all share is this dimensional place consisting of matter or physical form. In our metaphorical ecosystem of shared belief, culture creates matter. Believe it in your mind, and hold it in your hand, for what we believe- physics says we will achieve.

In our metaphorical ecosystem of shared belief, culture creates matter. – Culture Creates Matter

_____

_____

_____

_____

_____

_____

_____

_____

_____

_____

_____

_____

_____

_____

_____

_____

Do not forget to film a video!

Refer to page i for directions

Keep reading!
Keep writing!
Keep Filming!

DON'T FORGET TO FILM YOUR VIDEO!

Tag us when you're done!
 Culture Matters
 cultureunitesauthors

#thirtydaysofthought
#culturematters
#readwritespeak
#cultureunitesauthors

INDUSTRIAL AGE

Before connection there was inspection of industrial age of assembly and correction. We fell in line without purpose or foresight for a future we couldn't have dreamed possible. What has brought us together today doesn't matter. Our love, belonging and the belief of togetherness was not a factor then and every move we made, and all our thoughts were corrected.

During this feat of advancement, we came to resent the industrial age. Regardless of our mistakes in management and leadership we must be aware to the fact that times have changed. The dawn of connection is upon us. A sun beam of hope and fulfillment shines down in contrast to our past therefore, we must appreciate where we came from. The industrial age may have a bad "why," but with nine to five came ninety-five. Ninety-five is the hours of the entrepreneur, prerequisite to a new age of enlightenment when an age of information was an age of action. Without our ancestor's passion for freedom and desire for wealth and persistence in work, we would not be here today to pass judgment. Yes, culture does matter, and it is that precise fact why we must acknowledge our roots. With industry came pain, fear and anger, but also the steps to climb representing purpose, passion and love for our fellow men. We have climbed to the very top of limitations and it was this industrial age that came to birth our dreams. As Nietzsche said, "As I climb, a dog chases me, I call him ego." The culture of destiny is upon us solely due to these causes of trial. When we reminisce on our past and begin to pass judgment, let's make sure we take time to pause and appreciate. When we decide to learn from our past, we may earn dividends on our future. The industrial age has ended; learn, love and prosper as life happens with our minds in the past and our hearts in the future. The present does not become a gift unless we appreciate it and furthermore act upon it.

When we reminisce on our past and begin to pass judgment, let's make sure we take time to pause and appreciate. – Industrial Age

_____

_____

_____

_____

_____

_____

_____

_____

_____

_____

_____

_____

_____

_____

_____

_____

Do not forget to film a video!

LOVE

Without a shadow of doubt, love is what it's all about. A silly rhyme aside, my pen gently quivers as I write this. My heart on my sleeve, this pen is my weapon of choice to fight back ignorance, fear, pain and hatred. I see my reflection in my work. Only love may bring us joy, love itself knows no bounds. No word or phrase can contain it or explain it. It's anonymous, abstract, and unobservable. Love just is. So much love, I have inside of me, and as I write this I tear. No microphone, speakerphone or device will suffice. Love alone can save our human race. Love is pure; love is power for without love we can stand no more. What is love? That is the question. No answers may be found, and therefore love is scarce and knows no fear.

Friends, we joke and play at loves expense, we hope and pray for recompense. For life is love and love is life, it is the core value we share on the land that we live upon.

Love is leisure, liberty and lessons. The learning's of our failures and the legacy we leave behind from victories. If we don't open ourselves to love, we may never live. One could agree it's a blessing or a curse. We can be targets to the ill of the heart or the devil's keepers, but our love above that, can manifest destiny. Love is good, love is patient, and love is kind. Choose your power, my friend, and use your mind as I am writing this to you, my lover, my friend, as this pen touches parchment, I transfer my love to you. What is love? Love is life. Decide to live and you may never welcome strife.

For life is love and love is life, it is the core value we share on the land that we live upon. – Love

_____
_____
_____
_____
_____
_____
_____
_____
_____
_____
_____
_____
_____
_____
_____
_____
_____

Do not forget to film a video!

SIGNIFICANCE

Why do we struggle? Who are we fighting, if only against ourselves? Where are we going? When do we run out of time? These questions race through our minds and the answers to life may not have meaning as we feel out of time. Every ounce of our own personal being has been drained. I know this discomfort too well. I know you too well my brother, my sister, friend, foe, kinsmen, my life feels like it has been fulfilled for so long, but now with false pleasantries with a meaning null and void like a black hole of emptiness. Nothing will or has ever been enough. When I see my reflection looking back, I no longer can see myself. Who was I to begin with? Will I ever know my truth? Who is this stranger staring back at me? Day by day, as the clock ticks away, ticks getting louder and louder, I curl up on myself in deep-seeded emotion; hatred of whom I have become. I feel like a fraud to whom I know and who I am. It seems like it is all for nothing and that there is no point. Life has no destination but the one I have chosen. In a fleet of outer desperation, a claim to be the one worth loving beyond myself and beyond my safety net, woe is me and why can't I just be. Where is my glory? A salvation; my life's meaning and in times of trial I have asked myself why and only heard the beating of my own heart. It lies within, and it remains clear, yet the phrasing of the answer never comes. The only questions, however, are the ones invoked by unsettled emotion. Who am I? Where am I going? Will I ever be at peace? What is life's meaning? Without a sail, my ship is lost at sea and the sea so vast and boundless that its own existence only proves my worry. Will I ever know me…?

It's just a black mirror starring back at me with no answers and only questions. Quiet desperation fills the cloud I find myself on with self-constraint holding back my tears of outer self-pity and inner turmoil. Only you, black mirror, speak our inner thoughts. Only you.

Dedicated to Black Mirror

Life has no destination but the one I have chosen. – Significance

_____

_____

_____

_____

_____

_____

_____

_____

_____

_____

_____

_____

Do not forget to film a video!

Refer to page i for directions

Keep reading!
Keep writing!
Keep Filming!

DON'T FORGET TO FILM YOUR VIDEO!

Tag us when you're done!
 Culture Matters
 cultureunitesauthors

#thirtydaysofthought
#culturematters
#readwritespeak
#cultureunitesauthors

KNOW EVIL

The mirror is clear for it tells only truth. It is hard to hide one's secrets when facing them head on. As one contemplates life's virtues one has no other choice but to look inward as any other focal point shows only hollow ground to lay foundations of perspective. One's knees grow weak up to adherence of a counter to former logic. All misinterpretations, qualms, and unsettled thoughts result in non-conformity of self. When we do not allow our inner nature to take the lead, the perpetual sounding board plays violently within and opens the bottomless pit of self-gratification, hedonism, desire, dissonance, and evil. The evil we take for granted in the men and women who covet our prisons and labor camps- our corporate space. That evil is the demon of primal being. Pure evil is not pure; it is but an articulation of the essence of starved, cold, and hunter-like predators that lurk in our amygdala. We all share this devil- it is us and it becomes us when we think we are in control; this is our finest moment of self-intoxication. Contrary for us to know ourselves, we must know evil. How do we take heed of such signs of imperfections? We must start by looking in the mirror. To see through the titles placed upon our crest, we must recognize our fate and impose on our dark thoughts. We must allow our silent keeper to know who we are. We must know evil face-to-face as he lives in the reflection starring back. We must admit the truths, or we will know evil more than we know him today. Without recognition we are damned to become him- permanently.

How do we take heed of such signs of imperfections? We must start by looking in the mirror. – Know Evil

_____

_____

_____

_____

_____

_____

_____

_____

_____

_____

_____

_____

_____

_____

_____

_____

_____

Do not forget to film a video!

BORED

The greatest gift any creator may have granted us in his grace was that of boredom. To be cognizant of the development or lack thereof is solely a human element. The condition of a mind is affected by years of trial and error. Since the dawn of man before trees, and before we had the freedom, we demean today endless souls prevailed and collapsed for our right to be bored. This blessing of our nature is just one of many we have been granted with no will of our own invested, but we squander it and take it for granted. How lucky are we in fact to have such a choice, the right of man to be able to sit, think and feel? This is boredom by definition, and this is the result of the gift of life. All that can be understood is that to own our very nature and investing that into our here and now is a choice. This shows appreciation, gratitude and humility for our past, present and future. Heed my warning, be present and embrace life's struggle, and don't spit on the graves of your ancestors who died endlessly for your boredom. Be grateful.

Heed my warning, be present and embrace life's struggle… - Bored

_____

_____

_____

_____

_____

_____

_____

_____

_____

_____

_____

_____

_____

_____

Do not forget to film a video!

SELF-ACTUALIZED POKER FACE

When arising from pain and its counterpart, insecurity, one may become worthy through self-excellence, or practiced skill; interdependence at its finest hour. The illusive pursuit of a talent sharpened against endless hours of self-purgatory is the delusion of importance. Due to this self-absorbed cognition they in turn operate at a low frequency. This frequently exudes a false confidence but internally perpetuates self-doubt and insecurity. The mask of pride takes over its wearer and in turn disturbs all succumbed to this antagonist. When we are faced with foes of this nature our role must shift to that of water. Like water, we must flow based on our environment and who we meet day to day. Similar to life, water symbolizes us becoming our environment with its natural movement. In our life, our paths may be crossed by those whose character is solid, but consists of tar, a black substance consisting of vain behavior. This is plagued with ill notions of self and embodying a "hate-speak" concept for others. These lost souls are set in stone firmly ensconced in their self-gratification and will impose their negativity on others who are unable to fight back. They are our antagonists inculcated in the selfish and soulless embrace at skill of a craft, but blind to their disillusionment. Make sure to keep an open mind, heart and spirit for their encounters may crucify you or create you. Your inner power lies within; find it along with your confidence, competence, lovingness, and neutrality. Be water, my friend.

Dedicated to all the bullies, if you know one, have one or are one- read this and just let go…

Your inner power lies within; find it along with your confidence, competence, lovingness, and neutrality. – Self-Actualized Poker Face

_____

_____

_____

_____

_____

_____

_____

_____

_____

_____

_____

_____

_____

_____

_____

_____

Do not forget to film a video!

Refer to page i for directions

Keep reading!
Keep writing!
Keep Filming!

DON'T FORGET TO FILM YOUR VIDEO!

Tag us when you're done!
 Culture Matters
 cultureunitesauthors

#thirtydaysofthought
#culturematters
#readwritespeak
#cultureunitesauthors

LONESOME

The weight of the world weighs down on my shoulders, and every moment of every day the tasks at hand fill my mind. A faint whisper of "could be" and "should have" slithers into my ear lobes from my own negative thoughts bombarding my soul. As the hours drag on and the day passes it gets harder to subdue my demons. I feel filled with inner callings of fear, doubt, and restless thoughts of lonesome yet all I have now is a sharp blade of freedom due to my pen. The ability to choose in my current state presents two questions: Will I run and hide, or will I cut through my fears? Can I rely on my courage in times of self-reflection or on the contrary, doubt? As I ponder, I submit that the outcome of my decision is what matters most to me. Fame, glory, respect and admiration will constantly cloud my mind, so much that I will get ahead of myself. I am my own worst enemy and any facts that make me seem righteous, true, and courageous are but a travesty on my character. And due to the clarity of my pen, I cannot lie to you; I am a faker and a fraud. I am just the opposite of what I appear to be. Therein lies no heroics, no courage, no steadfast righteousness, no commitment, but only pride and entitlement. I am one to conjure up falsehoods to please only myself, and for that I am but a lonely man and I take responsibility.

The ability to choose in your current state presents two questions: Will you run and hide, or will you cut through your fears? – Lonesome

_____

_____

_____

_____

_____

_____

_____

_____

_____

_____

_____

_____

_____

_____

_____

_____

_____

Do not forget to film a video!

JUST OVER BROKE

The daily check-in had come. We counted our sheep and our dreams were had. At the break of dawn, we are awakened by the mechanical phoenix, flying into our perfect world of lavish halls and hearted romances. The clock strikes seven, the rooster calls, the phoenix rises, and we are back to reality. We are just over broke, and it is time for work. Our job has begun like the rising tide each one closer to the shore, then the last and every breath we take brings us closer to an attack. It is no wonder between 8AM and 9AM are deadly times as most suicides are dealt their hand between these hours. This is the dead zone where dreams are dreamt but never realized as they are seen in their nakedness, seen for the truth that they always are just dreams of an imagined mind. It's time to snap back into reality, it is 7:20AM now and time to get dressed. The next hours move fast as the kids tidy up for their illusion of future possibility. We shower, change, grab one spoon of what the progeny ate, after all we're second and they are first. And we're off. The rat race begins out of the driveway cognizant of our perfect neighbors, same house, same car, similar dream but exact embittered reality. Our least favorite time is upon us. The commute. So much for the longing of solitude our ride is riddled by horns, harassment and projection fouled upon us like invisible vomit. Each car a vessel for a love left behind, a dream forsaken, a song out of tune and a life unlived. The ride is our daily reminder of giving up. We are just over broke upon arrival to the spot with our name on it. Our name partly grayed from loiterers and time. Its letters stretched out like a mask placed perfectly over our face covering up who we are, the dreamer, the wonderer, the lover, the fighter, the possibility maker. We sigh, take our last breath, unfasten our seat belt, open our door and gather our belongings as one thought gathers our collective unconscious and it sounds like, "this is my last day being over broke." Your fate is up to you. Do something about it or just be comfortable being over broke.

To those living lives of desperation and hate your jobs, superiors and companies, keep reading and you will develop your light bright enough to quit. Masked as courage this is alignment with your genius and an inevitable end for those who are enough. Remain consistent and continue to read, write and speak every day.

Your fate is up to you. Do something about it or just be comfortable, "being over broke." – Just Over Broke

_____

_____

_____

_____

_____

_____

_____

_____

_____

_____

_____

_____

Do not forget to film a video!

DEATH AWAITS

He is thy enemy whether friend or foe faces him. Our greatest fear lies inside his cloak; the cape of chance. Unknown is the date of his arrival that of a meeting of death. Invisible to our naked eye are the exact origins of his power. Visible to all is the result of said will. His decisive hand bares down on us as a hammer cracks the edges of a nail. This nail placed precisely in our coffin whether friend or foe, common or uncommon majesty, or bank rolled or bankrupt. All men will await his fate. All men will cower in fear in sight of his presence only when known due to his cloak of chance disguising his grimace. Behind the hood he wears sits a smile so calm and the locked eyes of the focused hunter. He knows his task and his aim is exact. When our time has come, he does not waiver, he is the will and our power, he is source, he is home, and he is the end to our beginning. He is death, and neither friend nor foe, one cannot escape him. We must rejoice for every moment he has not been called to us. He is death. Rejoice and revel in his momentary absence. Friend or foe come to meet at common ground, death is not here he awaits but has no will for our ill fate therefore, rejoice. For in an instant his cloak of fate may appear, and it may all be lost. He is friend, foe, forced nature and will. He is power, he is death. Await his arrival at your own displeasure or bask in his absence, rejoice!

Dedicated to Sean Schellenger

When our time has come, he does not waiver, he is the will and our power, he is source, he is home, and he is the end to our beginning.
– Death Awaits

_____

_____

_____

_____

_____

_____

_____

_____

_____

_____

_____

_____

Do not forget to film a video!

Refer to page i for directions

Keep reading!
Keep writing!
Keep Filming!

DON'T FORGET TO FILM YOUR VIDEO!

Tag us when you're done!
Culture Matters
cultureunitesauthors

#thirtydaysofthought
#culturematters
#readwritespeak
#cultureunitesauthors

Life Is a Give and Take

Life is nothing but a give and take. The intent to give without expectation combined with willingness to take reparations. Without all parts the whole is nothing but imagination. An illusionary ideal of what could be with nothingness rooted in intangibility and fragmentation. Life is a give and take. When we cross the plane of ideals of imagined realities into a land of truism only two things matter: First, are we giving and second, have we made amends with taking. It may be difficult to juggle both; the yin and yang if you will. Some give freely while others take innately because after all, we are not cut from the same cloth. The facts, however, of this immortal life remains if we are to last forever in the memory of our brethren then we must be willing to give and to take. Life cannot go on without that balance. Non-alignment will plague our hearts, minds and spirits and all energy will be lost due to one giver giving and another taker solely taking. Equilibriums only ingredient is of itself rooted in its word, equal. Life is but a give and take so be open to serve, give and love whilst accepting your rewards. This reward is creation, and life is yours for giving and taking.

Dedicated to the acceptance of love.

Non-alignment will plague our hearts, minds and spirits and all energy will be lost due to one giver giving and another taker solely taking. – Life Is A Give and Take

_____

_____

_____

_____

_____

_____

_____

_____

_____

_____

_____

Do not forget to film a video!

PULLING THROUGH

Have you found your light? Yes? No? Maybe? The potential possibilities are infinite and the road to everlasting light toward a divine understanding of self; your personal power no one can steal. You have been traveling through the dark and grappling against the invisible reverberation of unseen power surrounding your entire being. Every day, you have read, written and spoken your truth into the ether. Every day you have conjured up new thoughts, untapped energy and dove head first into the dark to allow your light to shine; the beauty in your life founded by energy. This energy is manifested into words, thoughts and actions that affect you and everyone in your life. This habituation is that of light due to its reflection of your cosmogonic nature. You have the power to define your life, to refine who you are every day; a mind sun unbeknownst to power within the genius you reside over the writing to be uncovered...by you. Darkness only masks beauty, serenity and creativity. Darkness is only a source of power due to cosmic, biological, and psychological realities. All creation is birthed out of conflict. Conflict is the current, foreboding and all-encompassing darkness where life in and of itself is born. The light is you, and the light is us. Through this transcribed word, the excerpts you have read, written, and in return transmuted into your common tongue will be created through your conflict; your truth. For the last two weeks and forty-two excerpts your past self has been pushed to the surface, and thus new thoughts and opinions have been created. You are overcoming the dark and you have created new truths for yourself to be a better and brighter you. Do not give up as we are all interconnected, and you have meaning. You have contributed your light to our collective added consciousness; therefore, you are embedding wisdom into the future generations of the world, and therefore you have already changed the world. When you pull through, write your truth, and speak to the world through your darkness and conflict within, light will emerge. We, the human collective will reign free and you will be better for it. Thank you, my dark companion. Keep pushing through into the light.

From Caterpillar to Butterfly

We so easily limit ourselves and those around us with our perspective without the slightest realization of how we have come so far. Over the years our dearest friends or oldest lovers may forsake us. Their lack of belief in our current state says more about them than us, but could it be our metamorphosis? The journey we all partake in every day; from caterpillar to butterfly. As the caterpillar changes eventually into its prime we do not see, hear or feel anything due to the speed of the movement. And before we know it, the caterpillar is unrecognizable, and we turn back with regret or admiration.

When people transform it is those closest to them who may not always notice first since they are too close to see the transformation of growth. Therefore, we must remind ourselves to be fully present every time so those around us can see through their lens which may or not be clouded by their own cocoon.

The people we surround ourselves with will build us up or knock us down, and they might be a determining factor of whether we fly. There will be occurrences and there will be actions, there will be hurt and pain and these will restrict our wings, but restriction is not forever. Hurt, and pain is not eternity, but momentous and eclipsing. Evolution is infinite, and with evolution nothing or no one will prevent a purposeful butterfly to emerge from a caterpillar.

Restriction is not forever. – From Caterpillar to Butterfly

_____

_____

_____

_____

_____

_____

_____

_____

_____

_____

_____

Do not forget to film a video!

Conscious Thought = Internal Self- Culture

…I think I can…
……I think I can……
………I think I can………
…I know I can…
……I know I can……
………I know I can………
…I AM…

At the first sight of belief, the probability of being is created. This probable reality is an opportunity for our next conscious level of thought. Over time, these thoughts become truths and the truths we hold ever so tightly where we know them as our own. To know a truth for us ties to knots of persistent action which leads to results. The results that follow may be our prizes of life or failures but it's all about preparation. Regardless of what we think, know, do or become conscious thought is the fuel to our vehicles of reality; our internal self-culture. People are drawn to other passionate people who develop their purpose. Through purpose passion is demonstrated by representing character.

Character is shaped together like badges of honor or stripes of imprisonment. Our sets of values we hold is the meaning of the impact we have on others. These values must be understood to be set free.

Our conscious thought equals our internal self-culture which is our character everywhere we go and our light we shine on others into the hearts of our friends or foes. Character is internal self-culture, and it is our conscious duty in life to articulate our conscious thoughts powerfully because, culture matters.

People are drawn to other passionate people who develop their purpose. – Conscious Thought = Internal Self-Culture

_____

_____

_____

_____

_____

_____

_____

_____

_____

_____

_____

_____

Do not forget to film a video!

Refer to page i for directions

Keep reading!
Keep writing!
Keep Filming!

DON'T FORGET TO FILM YOUR VIDEO!

Tag us when you're done!
 Culture Matters
 cultureunitesauthors

#thirtydaysofthought
#culturematters
#readwritespeak
#cultureunitesauthors

HUMANITY

Oh, humanity! We, the wretched souls cower under the shadow of our past. We develop a false belief that all was true and all which we experienced has made us and defined us. We are not the happenings of life. We are not limited by occurrences caused by others, only by us. We are but the decisive habituations relegated unto us by our environment. The genes we have been impacted by our predecessors and the lucky happenstance we did not die as of moments passed. Humanity has drowned herself in a pool of woes, of dread, and the smog of desire has canvassed itself over her body of life with everlasting $H2O$; the essence of all beginnings. The birth of tragedy of this humanity is what we scrape off ourselves when we bathe and when we shed our primordial skin daily. When we reflect, grow and share our new truths with the ones who share this eco-system of belief called life. The culture we propagate and abstract within. Humanity is the culmination of every happening, all past occurrences (both energy and matter), the infinite future probabilities that are inevitable in this universe or another layered in between dimensionality. Humanity is every thought, idea, belief, action, ideology, dogma, culture, alignment, conflict, abundance, and interpretation of one's reality, both dissonant and corroborated by another. Humanity is birth and death, and culture is the expression of both into which we define our subjective into the agreed objective. Humanity is both described consciously and prescribed unconsciously by the collective social and spiritual consciousness, the driver of our will. This is a divine and human nature of things. When we think we know we do not understand and when we understand we know we do not know absolutely. These assertions are at the core of the matter, the humanity or the going under and the going over. Humanity is a tumult of conflict masked with aspirations and false altruistic tendencies perpetuated by hierarchical agreeableness. Done unto by way of watchers, followers and the masses, humanity, stop right there. Be righteous and pick your poison as we are all headed to the same place. All considered, life and death apparent, our transitions to new realms of reality and constant flux of who, what, why and where we are. We are thus spoken for and to. We are humanity.

Humanity is birth and death, and culture is the expression of both into which we define our subjective into the agreed objective. – Humanity

_____

_____

_____

_____

_____

_____

_____

_____

_____

_____

_____

_____

Do not forget to film a video!

Do You Want to be Managed?

"Mom!" "There is no way I am doing it!"

"Johnny, if you don't clean your room, you're grounded."

"But, Mom, it's my room, damnit!"

"What?!" "Did you just swear at me?" "Listen, if you don't clean your room, I am telling your Father."

Johnny sighs.

"Ahhhhhh… okay, I will do it"

Johnny utters under his breath.

"I freakin' hate her, why do I have to do this bull…"

And so, it goes on the daily struggles of life. The rooms left unkempt, the bed stays unmade, our tasks lay incomplete, and our relationships beguiled. What can we expect? After all, do you want to be managed?

Whether it is Mom, Dad, our lover or our boss, it appears someone is always telling us what to do: Who to date, how to live, where to go, what to do, or who to be. Early on, our self-significance is undervalued all the way up until our later years in life. From birth, we rely on our parents until old age when our caregivers watch our every move.

"Don't do this!" "Stop touching that" "Calm down!" "Speak up!" "Be Quiet!"

Oh, how we HATE being managed. It is no wonder why we loath 8AM. The alarm clock rings, we roll over in our perfect bed and say, "just a few more minutes" all the while knowing we *must* get up. We come to this conclusion not because it's righteous but due to conformity. We have succumbed to life's labors.

THERE MUST BE A BETTER WAY!

If there is not a better way, this vicious cycle will surely continue and for our full lifetime.

Well, let me let you in on a little secret- leadership is freedom and unshackles chains of conformity. Form the conscious and unconscious habit not to push, but to pull, stop telling, and start story telling. As a founder, parent, boss, lover and friend, it is your duty to pay careful attention to your light, your body giving it and every utterance of your vernacular conveyed, the difference between the influencer and the influenced lies in this understanding. If only Mommy knew.

"Mom! There is no way I am doing it!"

"Johnny, I hear you. Listen, love, I get it. When I was young, I didn't want to do it either, it sucks."

Mom continues...

"Can I ask you though, if you put it off now, would you have to do it later?"

"Yes, Mom."

Johnny thinks to himself, "Okay, that makes sense, eventually I will have to get it done."

His Mom continues...

"Friday, you have plans with Robby and Joey?"

"Yeah, Mom, I do."

"Ah, okay, I see you have a lot going on, a lot in your head and I imagine the last thing you want to do is clean. (pause) Although, wouldn't you rather do it now versus being late to your plans on Friday?"

Johnny thinks about that....

"Yeah, I didn't think about it that way. I will do it now."

"Thanks, Johnny, I love you."

"Love you too, Mom."

If only we knew our management was in our hearts and the key to its ignition is love, and the start of the ignition is perception. Every gallon of gasoline is our ability to listen, the pedal is understanding, and the clutch is all our questions.

Great leaders put themselves in other people's shoes. They feel their emotions, and they ask genuine questions to get down to the facts. Great leaders do not like to be managed, and they take that into account. After all, who likes to be managed, do you?

Leadership is freedom and unshackles chains of conformity. – Do You Want to be Managed

_____

_____

_____

_____

_____

_____

_____

_____

_____

_____

_____

Do not forget to film a video!

THE HOW

I have figured out "the how." It has been stated on more than one occasion that 80% of businesses fail within their first five years, and that of the 20% left, 80% of those fail within their first ten years! The fact is that all businesses will fail. The reasoning is not because of technological advances, nor compensation or capital costs, these are effects of an invisible cause, an amalgamation of factors. Systems, tools, technology, and products can always be replaced, but the soul of the company never has to be or should not be. The heart and essence of the company never needs to die yet, no matter the civilizations, ideologies, countries, and groups studied we will always find the same pattern. When the belief systems of the ecosystems die out, the businesses die too. We define culture as a metaphorical ecosystem of shared belief created by an influencer and maintained by the alignment of the influenced, and we know there is a tangible solution to keeping an organization alive forever. To keep the belief system alive forever, there must be values along with invisible architecture; the puzzle pieces of culture. The values must be found, transcribed, and done daily meaning, they need to be embedded onto the invisible and or visible collective or all-encompassing ethos of the group, inculcated and executed upon. This is the three-step linear process with a non-linear endpoint. How do we create alignment? How do we breathe life into an organization? The organizations teams should show up in purpose and inspired to learn to become the future leaders of said organizations, cultures and countries. "The how" comes from *how* clear the values are and *how* they are used to drive behavior with the results that follow. Leaders are to lead by figuring out why they founded their companies, groups or countries, how to transcribe their soul based on intrinsic values, and how to train their employees, soldiers, people, volunteers, and cultists through those values so the production comes from purpose allowing the original culture to live, develop and expand forever. For a belief system to last forever your culture must matter. Let us show you how…

See The Culture Puzzle, coming soon out of The Collective

Systems, tools, technology and products can always be replaced, but the soul of the company never has to be or should not be. – The How

_____

_____

_____

_____

_____

_____

_____

_____

_____

_____

_____

_____

Do not forget to film a video!

Refer to page i for directions

Keep reading!
Keep writing!
Keep Filming!

DON'T FORGET TO FILM YOUR VIDEO!

Tag us when you're done!
f Culture Matters
@ cultureunitesauthors

#thirtydaysofthought
#culturematters
#readwritespeak
#cultureunitesauthors

SYSTEMS DON'T REPLACE PEOPLE

What is man? Man is unlimited potential meant to be cultivated. Like a summer harvest potential may draw rich crops, but depending on man's maker, riches can be lost. Systems don't replace people. As tactics in planting may increase yield, yield is still a determining factor of love and the destiny of care. This connection between maker and man is to farmer and crops as to manager and managed. When we treat our people without tender and care our harvest will not reap and we will never foresee systematic results. Our future is bleak, and no matter what seeds we sow, our harvest will be full of fear, anger and doubt. Man is love, and man is thought. When he feels no love, he has no thought. Without thought there is no creation and creations are the birthplace of innovation. In an ever-evolving world of trial and error and of creation, we must cherish man and inspire thought.

A system is not a person; it is an action and therefore an effect. Science says that effect cannot replace the cause, and in this case, the cause is man and the cause is thought. People become their thoughts that are cleansed, or become void of toxins based on the culture they are in. When man's maker is focused on systems he is not focused on cultivating man. This is what leads to zero innovation and what ultimately causes societies, groups, families, companies, cultures and all ecosystems to die. Man's potential is its unmeasured scope that only becomes measured based on their respect for their maker. Are men respected as much as systems? Are we more concerned with numbers and systems or thought? Systems cannot and do not replace people. Take heed of your conscience after digesting this outcry, it will not lie to you as much as yourself or man.

Without thought there is no creation and creations are the birthplace of innovation. – Systems Don't Replace People

_____

_____

_____

_____

_____

_____

_____

_____

_____

_____

_____

Do not forget to film a video!

ATTENTION DEFICIT

His hands are sweaty with his palms steadily losing grip of the pen in hand as thoughts creep in. These ideas lack focus for the topic at hand, and their aim is not to interrupt, but to interpret observations of information. No one in his shoes could ever understand. All at once, every sensory emotive stance is triggered in his cortex. Although we cannot see inside his mind, it lights up and imagination is birthed like a new born sun. All matter around this light gets the energy needed to grow. Unfair to this man, a miracle in presence with his inner nature, yet his untapped potential- no one ever understands. They underestimate him, they call him names, and they condescend and attempt to label him. Due to their own misguided love, and their ignorance to his genius they portray him to others and himself as crazy. He is confused to social hierarchy; a misunderstood creative that is misinformed and untapped in his creativity. He is labeled, ADHD. This man was the next creator; he was an inventor, and a noble prize winner waiting to be heard. No one will trump his voice. He stands when their pen is loose in grip, when their answers are wrong, and their writing misses the mark. He yells, clearly, the answer of a question never asked. No one knows his genius, but he is asked politely to sit down. A man of talent hits the mark others miss but a man of genius sees the mark no other can see. And thus- he is medicated.

Dedicated to: The labeled, those called out, forsaken and forgotten, do not submit. Be unique and unleash your true genius for inequality reigns supreme. Please share to spread hope.

Although we cannot see inside his mind, it lights up and imagination is birthed like a newborn sun. – Attention Deficit

_____

_____

_____

_____

_____

_____

_____

_____

_____

_____

_____

Do not forget to film a video!

KNOWLEDGE IS
POTENTIAL ENERGY

Knowledge is an everlasting flame. This flame burns bright in a place that cannot be seen, yet once we meet its blaze it cannot be unseen. The act of knowing is potential energy because in between what can be and what will become is based on a decision. We are the master, the creator and the determining factor of all possibilities. The adage that knowledge is power is false. For only the creator behind such potential may put Newton's laws into motion.

Firstly, it must be the action that has every reaction. As the pendulum of life swings, we ask ourselves, why? The answer is complex; the decision based off the knowledge or potential energy started the swing in the first place. Awareness instigates life swinging and the test both good and evil perceives one's self. We are the knowledge and according to how we choose to apply it makes us the power. We are merely defining ourselves. When we define our being, we open the potential to refine our behavior. Life is a marathon to our own soul and our mind is the door we must walk through to gain new realities to manifest.

Knowing grants permission and permission leads to decision. Decision in comparison to your metaphorical vehicle can be your stick shift, brakes or ignition. Decisions will change, decisions will be put on hold or decisions will go full throttle, and your knowledge will be the fuel. All potentials have a starting point in another reality as energy is not destroyed, but only displaced and replaced. We must overcome our arrogance of self before we can replace old thoughts with the new. To become our best, we must self-discover. The ecosystems we create in our universe lie in our hands between our words and our will to tap into information with the ability to let out energies of every beam of sunlight within us.

If knowledge is power and knowledge is enough, then we are already dancing stars. Our children are self-aware and self-actualized, plagues of ill will and suffering are a far cry from reality and ignorance is read about in books of an older age. If this is not our current state of reality then knowledge is not your power, but knowledge is your potential power. We must become aware and start tapping into its untold powers of love, peace, joy and abundance. Knowledge is potential energy, and we are that power. Unleash your power with decision.

We are the knowledge and according to how we choose to apply it makes us the power. – Knowledge is Potential Energy

_____

_____

_____

_____

_____

_____

_____

_____

_____

_____

_____

_____

Do not forget to film a video!

Refer to page i for directions

Keep reading!
Keep writing!
Keep Filming!

DON'T FORGET TO FILM YOUR VIDEO!

Tag us when you're done!
Culture Matters
@cultureunitesauthors

#thirtydaysofthought
#culturematters
#readwritespeak
#cultureunitesauthors

BEING DIFFERENT

The difference between a smile and a frown are as contrasting as Pluto and its sun, the warmth of acceptance and the frozen chill of ambivalence. When we are left out far from our colleagues, the crowd never feels like quite enough. At times of acceptance a shield of love protects us and guards our hearts from our greatest enemy, ourselves. To be different is a blessing in the right of truth, but a curse in the solidarity of having to be just that; different. When you walk amongst the "yes man", and exist with the herd, a subtle yet stinging lonesome feeling creeps up your spine. The feeling of awkward imprisonment within a cage of insignificance rushes around your mind like an aura of judgment forsaking your every thought. Fear of non-conformity plays at every game your mind takes part in and being different is a plague spread through your essence. Please just know upon digestion and upon your journey when you arrive at this point, you are not alone. I am here staring back at you. I know your fear, and I know your pain, and you do not have to be afraid anymore. This self-infliction and pain must be put to rest. Believe you are different, understand you are different, because being different will set you apart from everything that is mundane, and I will be your friend. I am your higher nature, I am your better self, I am on the other side of decision. My name is, "smile," and I am here to light up the universe with your story. Onlookers and passerby's alike will be inspired by me, by you, and by us. Our aura will brighten up our world. Be different for you, me and everyone longing in the darkness.

To be different is a blessing in the right of truth. – Being Different

_____

_____

_____

_____

_____

_____

_____

_____

_____

_____

_____

_____

Do not forget to film a video!

SOULMATE

A lifetime may pass without any formal recognition by society of our one true love. This non-sympathetic appropriation of love and belonging centered around, "tying the knot" or getting married. The ideal of two intertwined into one welcoming life and death in a long embrace plagues those who feel lost. We are forced to believe in what may not hold true that we must fall in love. We are blind in a sense of ignorance to what we have proven without doubt. We are all connected by desire and survival, and the notion of love falls by the wayside to those who see the light. A symbolic candle is lit with emotion and rationale by those who take the efforts to become aware of the science of the survival of the fittest; a fight or flight misfiring of Darwinian understanding. We are mammals at our core, animalistic in nature and selfish in charm. Our nature is deeply riddled with self-infatuation and an indulgence of self-importance. This biology courses through our veins and may be distinguished from societal illusion leaving us to wonder if love is dead. The idea of love and that we all must find our yin to our yang is nothing but a common mis-understanding of self. Love yourself, and that shall set you free from any burden brought unto you by an ideal of ever needing another. A soulmate... If not? What do I know of love? I am but a reader, a writer, a lost soul, and a speaker. A speaker lost in endless squabble and thought provocation forever alone stuck in the dark and perpet-ually damned yet eager to bask in sunlight. In my lonesome, and in my pain, I have found solace. I have made conflict masked as passion my mate, and in that I am my own soulmate. I am in love with myself. How damned am I?

Love yourself, and that shall set you free. – Soulmate

_____

_____

_____

_____

_____

_____

_____

_____

_____

_____

_____

_____

Do not forget to film a video!

CULTURAL ALIGNMENT

Word-Thought Matrix (WT-M) is the words people say, thoughts people have, ideas that come from those thoughts and the new actions that are taken. Those actions create outcomes, and this is where cultural alignment is integral because this is where fear sets in. False evidence appearing real is where people quit. Thus, entropy persists. The invisible lasso of our cultural commune, humanity takes hold and causality affects effectuality. This is the WT-M. When the WT-M affects people, their words, thoughts, ideas and actions change in self and in their environment. The WT-M is people. We are our thoughts. They keep going while new beliefs form which over time become unconscious habits. Those habits change their state which changes their story and they become convicted. Convicted people are what we call leaders. These leaders have a new purpose through their results of not quitting, and they exude passion. They are shining bright as the stars they are, engulfed in purpose. The words they say along with the thoughts they hold bring new actions, beliefs, habits and convictions. Convictions create cultures. The result is cultural alignment, and this is what creates matter which is relative to actions that are systematic and repeated to get results through all material systems or the physical world. Cultural alignment plus our systems squared create success to any outcome whether positive or negative. Culture creates matter due to curiosity plus focus multiplied by grit, squared equals success because when we define it, we control it. Within this control lies power. We call this power, freedom to decide. In decision lies creation due to our WT-M. Vision is the visual explanation of the founder's purpose and mission is what must be done to accomplish it. Values are the founders or leader's character delineated into contextual energy with sustainable actions for followers to grow into offspring of the founder or leader. This creates cultural alignment which is when everyone is in frequency magnifying the results on all spectrums to make sure systems are completed daily. Thus, the founder or leader is not working in the business, but on the business. Cultural alignment is what changes the employees and leaders WT-matrices into where it needs to specialize and indoctrinate everyone in the company on whatever doctrine is required. This is all done by finding it, transcribing it and then doing it daily by training and deliberately aligning your organization, company, group, country or any society's culture, because culture creates matter. The bridge from one culture to the other is alignment and this more than anything matters. Yours, mine and every human's WT-Matrix is reliant upon it for the good in and of us all.

Convictions create culture. – Cultural Alignment

_____

_____

_____

_____

_____

_____

_____

_____

_____

_____

_____

Do not forget to film a video!

Refer to page i for directions

Keep reading!
Keep writing!
Keep Filming!

DON'T FORGET TO
FILM YOUR VIDEO!

Tag us when you're done!
 Culture Matters
 cultureunitesauthors

#thirtydaysofthought
#culturematters
#readwritespeak
#cultureunitesauthors

FINDING CULTURE

How do we find culture?

The importance of "being" in any scenario determines its potential to act upon the "knowing". Therefore, when we develop a definition to something, we organize its meaning into a context of understanding that we may need to attain and repeat certain results. When the subject of culture arises this amorphous blob of rhetoric surely glides over all surveyors' heads. The common misunderstanding is that "culture" is a noun; however, on the contrary it is not. Culture is a non-physical state of being. You see, we all have a culture- a metaphorical ecosystem of shared beliefs we have articulated upon to form our matrix of reality. As soon as we let our guard down, we either influence other spiritual body sacks for or against our beliefs. Our body sacks are what covers up our spiritual essence and essentially what we define as our individual culture or self. This internal, but metaphorical ecosystem of shared belief which is created by an "influencer" we call body sack, is us. Unfortunately, not created solely by us, but free will is a topic for another discussion. When it comes to answering the question, "what is culture?" context is important in determining the following: culture of self, culture of many or cultural alignment. For all intents and purposes to this writing, we will define culture in the context of "cultural alignment" as that is the relevant term in relation to influencing more than one organism or spiritual "body sack" if you will.

Culture being created by an influencer and maintained by the collective alignment of the influenced is vital in understanding to then partake in the necessary actions to execute cultural alignment. Our shared belief is something we cannot touch, yet still lives with every passing breath, thought, word, and group activity shared. This ecosystem is the involvement of more than one self being observed and being the observer of relationships. At one point in time, our self-culture could be influencing or under the act of being influenced by an outside force. Our inner world is either the cause or effect of our outer world.

The second part of our newly forming definition of culture has to do with ours or others ability to convey their self-culture. Please note that there is <u>always</u> an influencer no matter the circumstance; the salesperson and the customer, the manager and their employee, the parent and their off-spring- the influencer is always doing the creating and the influenced is always doing the maintaining. The irony in this explanation is the influencer does not always have to be the positional leader, or in other words, who you may expect to be the influencer in general life. For example, the best salesperson on the team, whom everyone gets along with may not be the boss but still empowers and influences daily to the rest of the team they are a part of. Another example would be a manger who constantly heckles his/her staff and condemns their tactics, yet the salesperson pays zero attention to their manager. The culture is aligned in favor of the salesperson versus their manager, because the influenced or people respects the salesperson.

The third part of the definition is about those who are influenced; the followers. The followers are who hold the invisible glue which then holds the non-physical ecosystem together. We must remember during this stage to tread lightly and the safe factors we use to strengthen may end up destroying. The words we use, the actions we take and the character we uphold are paramount to the factors that determine whether we are influenced or influential. Before we can mold people, and become fair and direct in our circumstance, we must redefine culture, so we can refine our behavior. Culture is not found but created through the word of the influencer along with invisible architecture and maintained with permission from both the conscious and unconscious hearts, minds and spirits of the influenced. Create your culture and define yourself.

Read more in Book six, The Culture Puzzle

Culture is not found but created through the word of the influencer and maintained with permission from the conscious and unconscious hearts, minds and spirits of the influenced. – Finding Culture

_____

_____

_____

_____

_____

_____

_____

_____

_____

_____

_____

_____

_____

Do not forget to film a video!

Refer to page i for directions

Keep reading!
Keep writing!
Keep Filming!

DON'T FORGET TO FILM YOUR VIDEO!

Tag us when you're done!

Culture Matters

cultureunitesauthors

#thirtydaysofthought
#culturematters
#readwritespeak
#cultureunitesauthors

My Comrades

This love I owe to you my fellow comrades, we can stand tall with our chests puffed out with pride knowing we have served. If we died today no one could say we had been selfish. Self-serving aims are the target of our weapons and these battle fields are a nasty place to go toward alone. As I sit, I have my pen in hand and I reminisce the times of our past. Solo in my strife and multiple in my problems, it is only me, myself and I hell bent to overcome them. Now you are here beside me and together we know no evil, no fear only greatness. We will be victorious. When times get tough, I have you to share my burdens with. Shoulder to shoulder we march arms hooked around one another. Regardless of mental or emotional state, we are here for each other and I love you, my comrades, and my friends. Together we will rise or fall, but my trust is in you, my heart is here for you, and my mind is yours. We have proven that happiness for a lifetime means to help somebody else. Together we can hear the beat of victory play louder as our bond grows stronger. We must never look back. Our only chance at success lies on the others willingness to understand each other and our passion. Brothers and sisters, I love you. Amen.

We have proven that happiness for a lifetime means to help somebody else. – My Comrades

_____

_____

_____

_____

_____

_____

_____

_____

_____

_____

_____

Do not forget to film a video!

L.O.V.E

Discard all infatuation with thyself, push away all thoughts of "I," "my," or "me," and embrace "we," "our" and "us." Choose to become plural and you will know the word, LOVE. Lead – Others – Virtuously – and into Eternity. Leading starts with acceptance of the plural ideal. The thought that it is not "me," but it is "we." Leadership starts with a look in the mirror at self and reflection upon the current track the beholder is facing. Ask the perfect questions that open awareness to self and open doors to a richer, more joyous and socially agreeable life not of just one but many. This new sense of discovery cannot take change without more than one. Therefore, leading others becomes a natural path into "V," virtuously. The guiding post for all behavior decision and culture is our virtue. Virtue may be the bedrock of our social faith and the glue that holds the "me" to the "we." Transcribe your virtue clearly, concisely and use the work written and spoken to enroll your fellow man into leadership. Guide them through love by leading others virtuously through your selfishly selfless axioms imprinted into your and their minds daily. For this will lead to our last word, "eternity." Long after your temporary form is gone your virtue may hold attention to who you are and set it in stone as a guiding light to lead others virtuously and with eternity in mind. Even after the "you" that was the "I" and "me" you let go is long gone and what will last is your LOVE. Love embodies the energy fragments of the leadership of others through virtue and for all eternity. Just be a "we" and not a "me." Be L.O.V.E.

Virtue may be the bedrock of our social faith and the glue that holds the "me" to the "we." – L.O.V.E

_____

_____

_____

_____

_____

_____

_____

_____

_____

_____

_____

_____

Do not forget to film a video!

LIFE AFTER DEATH

As our hearts make way to their final beat, and our eyelids weigh heavy we recognize that these final moments are when we are going to ask ourselves if there is life after death. Does the dawn set on my soul? In reflection and thought, I feel what it means to be me is so dear. The attachments I have made, the melodies that have been sung, the tunes I have heard, times of laughter, times of turmoil and how I have risen above it all by digging deep to form my purpose. We never will let up because it matters, because culture matters. Without answers or the hope in a better tomorrow there is only doubt and a lonely mind of empty regrets by a selfish me. The cycle of living is here and now and without hope in life there is no reason to fight anymore. The notion of transition is what gives us our strength to make us whole and without the sure signs of life after death there could be no cause to battle on. Our struggle in transition comes from the empty voids we must fill to feel fulfilled. The reality is that dying is easy and living is hard. As our hearts beat the last few rhythms and we drift off to sleep for our last dream, we may realize that we are just then finally about to wake up.

The notion of transition is what gives us our strength to make us whole and without the sure signs of life after death there could be no cause to battle on. – Life After Death

_____

_____

_____

_____

_____

_____

_____

_____

_____

_____

_____

_____

Do not forget to film a video!

Refer to page i for directions

Keep reading!
Keep writing!
Keep Filming!

DON'T FORGET TO FILM YOUR VIDEO!

Tag us when you're done!
f Culture Matters
⊙ cultureunitesauthors

#thirtydaysofthought
#culturematters
#readwritespeak
#cultureunitesauthors

PUBLIC ORATION

When it comes to speaking, we are not created equal. Brash claims such as these never fall on deaf ears therefore, I plead my case and do not confuse equal with fair. The equality of the matter we will leave up to the great unknown as only it has the answer for that because it is out of our control. The masses do not commit, whether they are aware or unaware is unfortunately irrelevant to the case that in times like these they can, will and should have the opportunity to speak. The beauty in our times is that men, women and children can speak their truth. This truth is a wave length drifting into the invisible eco-system of shared or unshared atmospheres of those able to interpret it. This perspective able to be heard, absorbed, and processed into tangible data is information capable of causing rapid change. The only solution to this being interpreted well is how it is deconstructed to make a clear sound. Wisdom is determined by reflection or the sole proprietor of thought. To abundantly add value through oratory we must follow the formula for greatness; read plus write, plus speak. For without the latter or the former, we, as the proposed influencer are not deserving of the outcome, to speak well. We are coalesced in a world view held together by science and the methods of intellectual reasoning. There is proof that this formula works. In moments, we will see that those who get the passage to speak may not give any new truth or real value and only speak due to their own arrogance instead of interest in selfish-selflessness or even biology. Unfortunately, these people are unconsciously incompetent with, "what they don't know, they don't know," and are just lost souls looking for meaning, mulling around with humble words yet megalomaniacal behavior. This causes chaos and disorder of social consciousness and although some chaos is necesssry, in order to speak a clear message filled with wisdom- order is advised. Continue reading, writing and speaking daily for then your words will pack wisdom glittered in gold. Their color will shine bright and light up the eyes of onlookers inspired to live and let live!

We will see that those who get the passage to speak, may not give any real value and only speak due to their own arrogance instead of interest in selflessness or even biology. – Public Oration

_____

_____

_____

_____

_____

_____

_____

_____

_____

_____

_____

_____

Do not forget to film a video!

THE CONCEALED TRUTH

The abundance of truth that lives underneath our surface far exceeds the observable innateness of its misguiding endeavor. The truth that conceals itself is love. Hidden away, buried under layers upon layers of experience the truth awaits its slumber. The dragon of chaos breaths fire and guides the grander treasure within. Underneath our scaly armor those false representations of strength, the prideful gestures of defense, the opaque smiles and the quid pro quo behaviors mask our truth. Bureaucracy trumps intimacy and our dragon of chaos has a heartbeat, and its only her fiery breathing shut off and distant from her truth that her real treasure lies unveiled. Her heart is asleep the truth is masked, and the treasures of life are lost. Fallen into the depth of imagination for life's meaning is found in our awakening we must be open to each other, our own reflection and the dark dragon of chaos that is concealing the truth, our heart and our love. Only one truth cannot be concealed, love, for it represents all that is open. Your fire awaits when you awaken. It is purpose.

The dragon of chaos breaths fire in its slumber and guide the grander treasure within. – The Concealed Truth

_____

_____

_____

_____

_____

_____

_____

_____

_____

_____

_____

_____

Do not forget to film a video!

1,000,000 SUPERMEN ACTING AS ROBIN

'Twas the night before dawn, the dawn of man, man's awakening, and his birthright had given maladjusted in, with his eyes wide. The groggy, copasetic ambivalence to his better, higher, grander nature subdued by happenstance and circumstance. This man; superman, born into stimulus limiting, disheartening, and silenced of his genius is stalled out and gives in to what is easy; Robin. Robin is a representation of his second-best self, rather than his maximum potential, he lives in minimal effort. His genius potential and genius stuck in neutral is locked in gear. That is Robin; a man's second-best self, masked and too insecure to face the truth. His unknown kryptonite is his ultimate fear to face the facts, the environment stopped him. Robin the false superman knows not himself for the letting go of pain and internal strife. Confidence and grief are contrasted by a mask he wears for others. He is but a daring hero held in the gravity of his own sun with the feeling of potentially never-ending conflict and loneliness. He cannot make it out of his own way. All of that stated formally, a recompense not of his birthright- his genius within God given and self-emancipated by freedom but perpetrated by the fact he was born under probabilistic conditions. Unwilling to face the facts, he is a product of his environment and a fake man or "fake alpha." He endures weak minds which causes tainted hearts and egos that thrust out into a skewed view portrayed for wise men to feed these mask wearing Robins, and they are liars. They use their loved ones, in fact they know not love, therefore superman is but a noun to be sought out in a novel, not of themselves, a person, not a place they can know and thus a thing unimaginable for them. They are cut off, limited, masked, un-enthralled by curiosity, undeserving and non-observant. One million supermen who have the power, hold the key to life; the castle in the corner of the sky, and not the key to their entire world, why? The mask of insecurity is much too heavy, and real negative emotions and impartial bias to love will, can and does hold back men of Robin. For this their void can never be filled thus they stay number two into infinitum, second to the best of themselves, perpetually self-reliant and independent. These fake men with quiet, unloved and forthright lives of desperation impact all those who cross their paths. Robin is a dancing star, yes of course man is man that of genius, that of superman, but he may never know it due to causes of stimulus of environment and for that there are 1,000,000, supermen operating as Robin...... Those dancing stars at night, and we will never see their dawn.

Dedicated to a dear client and even dearer friend, I have grown through your growth and that is the meaning of life.

Robin is a dancing star, yes of course man is man that of genius, that of superman, but he may never know it due to causes of stimulus of environment and for that there are 1,000,000, superman operating as Robin. – 1,000,000 Supermen Acting as Robin

_____

_____

_____

_____

_____

_____

_____

_____

_____

_____

_____

_____

Do not forget to film a video!

Refer to page i for directions

Keep reading!
Keep writing!
Keep Filming!

DON'T FORGET TO FILM YOUR VIDEO!

Tag us when you're done!
Culture Matters
cultureunitesauthors

#thirtydaysofthought
#culturematters
#readwritespeak
#cultureunitesauthors

Two Forks

We all face decisions in life and come to two forks to choose from. This metaphorical cross road for our individual journey's has completely different outcomes and its words we tell ourselves moment by moment that create the vicious cycles of mediocrity or success. This imaginary left fork is the route to selfishness, self-loathing, predominant inebriation and all things we tend to "climb up hill" to attain. This left fork is alluring, exciting and cool. The left fork is the easy road. For too long I had my right foot where I was supposed to be, the right fork, that road to enlightenment and what is possible. However, my left foot was dug deeply into the left fork. Every inch I stepped out of that left fork was a fight and when I thought I had control is exactly when I had the least power internally and externally. The destinations of where we end up are either our own or that of forces, we cannot control pending our footing we can own a more provocative stance that we dominate. We talk about a sense of knowingness but if this is true why do so many not reach it? The answer is they are stuck in the abyss. This abyss I speak of is where our dreams never come into fruition. The place life's curiosity dies, and anger, self-loathing and resentments lie. The abyss is the origin of all life's woes due to every one of us not finding our right path or deciding to not fully commit. When we go through life with even a toe still in the "left fork" with all the intention being in the right fork, our dreams will never come true. The only solution to this problem resides in you, but only when ready to see its horizon beyond the pain, discomfort and harsh reality that has been; you have not been authentic. Truly all abundant experiences in life come from stepping every inch of one's mind, body, soul and intention out of this metaphorical "left fork" thrusting one's entire energy forces into the right fork of life. Make the choice to go all in, burn all the ships behind you, start taking responsibility for whatever outcome may unfold, and just go after purpose with no distractions. If you are not sure of what this "purpose" truly is stay tuned I will share with you mine ….

Make the choice to go all in, burn all the ships behind you, start taking responsibility for whatever outcome may unfold, and just go after purpose with no distractions. – Two Forks

_____

_____

_____

_____

_____

_____

_____

_____

_____

_____

_____

_____

Do not forget to film a video!

Culture of Obscurity Is Over but It's Up to You...

Obscurity is defined as a state of being unknown or inconspicuous and unimportant. This word has no value to the individual, family or nation being that we are all a race of "socialites" and quantifiable as any social organism. In an age where everything may be a click away, we are a moment from obscurity, but more importantly a millisecond from familiarity. Acceptance is a root in esteem and esteem is a pillar of survival, Abraham Maslow had it laid out for us clearly, the question we must answer is, "do we know enough to take advantage?" Tangibly we live in an age where we have the resources to define our individual culture. Our individual culture makes us who we are to the world and expresses our inner self-actualization. Now answer yourself this question, if you're one of the many entrepreneurial types who has stumbled upon your "purpose" and are aware of your "culture," are you utilizing the age of informational democracy and abundance? Are you properly sharing the "culture" you have inside your being with the world? Using myself for example, I am a curious being, a thinking orator, a being screaming to give and attain love through these actions and habits. The purpose I serve lights me up like a firestorm, and when I serve my purpose on the daily goose bumps line my arms down to my feet. To live in alignment, I must do the following: read, write and speak every day. Why? Because, I am creating new purpose every day. Whether you are the sun already, shining bright or creating a life of purpose there is one truth that remains; the digital age has given us a gift not to be pure selfishness. Are you putting yourself out there? If I read every day, I must post it, so others know what to read. When I write every day, I am willed to share it, so others may think, it's a responsibility. After speaking every day, I vow for myself and the world to record it, so others may hear and let their dreams take flight. For my purpose ripens with getting started by following the Facebook Five(www.culturematterscourses. com) which gave me life. As I write this excerpt, the year is 2018, the age is of information, and the word is obscurity and the meaning: obscurity is the devil and the heavens *can* win. Be your own guardian, and let your voice be heard for the culture of obscurity is over but it's up to you... Be light! Shine like the sun you are.

Dedicated to the culturites, individuals who read, write and speak their thoughts inspired by Culture Matters.

Our individual culture makes us who we are to the world and expresses our inner self-actualization. - Culture of Obscurity is Over but It's Up to You

_____

_____

_____

_____

_____

_____

_____

_____

_____

_____

_____

_____

Do not forget to film a video!

HEAT

Heat is the embodiment of hard work. A blanket of perspiration glistens his back as beads of sweat ball up to form a mass. This watery sheath covers him and makes him uncomfortable, but nonetheless he knows what it takes. Success is slippery, so much it tends to slip through many of hands. He is proud of himself; he is aware of what is, and the fact remains, most people fail. They don't succeed, they cannot bare the sweat, and they can't take the heat! The former, a symbolic transformation of a battle fought hard. A battle primordial in nature and one pitted in his deepest, darkest and unconscious identity. A battle of the conscious mask he wears juxtaposed to this invisible strife externally and as he climbs in his personal development that of his higher self, a dog chases him symbolic of his ego. The primitive word speaks unto him, his conscious mind and whispers of fear and doubt while spitting up inklings of hesitation. Disease plagues his mind as he walks toward his aim. Although his eyes are focused with his prize in clear sight something holds him back. This occurrence is a natural process and an undergoing of development. A demon he must face presents itself at the beginning, middle and end of each endeavor. After all, this is well sprung. Heat, fire and brimstone pollute the eyelids of his looking glass and he sees nothing but smoke and mirrors. He must face his truth with all that he knows for he can no longer wait. He must work under pressure. After all, this explanation, depiction and explicit erudition can never be expressed. This is life. This is hell. Can you stand the heat?

Dedicated to Marc F.

Heat is the embodiment of hard work. – Heat

_____

_____

_____

_____

_____

_____

_____

_____

_____

_____

_____

Do not forget to film a video!

Refer to page i for directions

Keep reading!
Keep writing!
Keep Filming!

DON'T FORGET TO FILM YOUR VIDEO!

Tag us when you're done!
 Culture Matters
 cultureunitesauthors

#thirtydaysofthought
#culturematters
#readwritespeak
#cultureunitesauthors

REBORN

The sun is hell- visually blinding, atmospherically incomprehensible to all life on earth. No sounds may be uttered nor heard. Senses do not sense in the brimstone and fire erupting, vulcanizing, blazing, churning, flaring and burning within the heat of our star. The hell off earth that makes heaven and hell on earth possible is the same dancing star that makes you, love, and the creation and maintenance of life possible. The sun proves to us on all universal, physical, cosmological, biological, neurological, psychological, and sociological levels. Historically, life and creation results from conflict. One clear beginning of life is your sun, and our sun, hence why "son" in the English language is the meaning of a new life being born. As the cycle of life continues, rebirth is about understanding that you are on a material, visual, and pragmatic level. It is abstract, but empowering. *You* are the sun of *your* own solar system. Conflict is light collocated by dark and becomes a better and worse nature at odds; the angel on one shoulder and the devil on the other. This ultimately creates human discussion about internal conflict that we all share in our own way; a universal pact we have made to grapple with our energy source of darkness. As we continue, we learn that through the darkness comes our light. Our light will continue to fight the gravitational pull of the unknown, not in place but in movement staring back at us blankly. The rays of our energy are what we use to mirror the sun's life on a micro level and therefore meaning is created by us and through us. The sun is our parent and we are its sons and daughters all at once. We are constantly, perpetually, and infinitely yet finitely in purpose shining our light on all who will take heed. The outcome of the equation is rebirth; an understanding of its physics. Energy is never gone, but solely displaced and replaced. The sun is energy, you are the sun and this book you have been digesting while conflicted with transcribing inside and verbalizing outside is a tiny metaphor for our parents' similar battle with the cosmos. By now you are culture shocked, some of your walls have come down and in that process of deconstruction, and new thought, energy, opinions and arguments have come to surface. As you spend your days reading, writing and speaking, the time came to "pull through," and a small amount of your light was peaking its tiny head from your eternal and intrapsychic womb. As the weeks go by in a new alchemical design to your inner and outer being is a mastery of your own mind. You are reading deeper, thinking higher and denser, and for the first time your thoughts are not difficult to articulate. The videos shared, filmed and unscripted with banter have left your mind and started to shine into the darkness of others. The space between your opinions and theirs has made you brave again as if back in adolescence when speaking your truth was as simple as just saying so. For the first time, you can speak up unencumbered by others and yourself with confidence to reply with conviction. First, you were shocked, and then you pulled through, now you are a new you still conflicted yet understanding of your conflict. You are at peace with the missing piece you are still uncovering. You are now reborn, and action is the only thing that matters. You are in your "now." You appreciate the darkness, and you will continue to read, write and speak daily while sharing what you have created. Continue to act because part of harnessing the dark to enable your light knows that we will always have some conflict and we want to, because from conflict there is creation. You are now reborn. Bless you, for being reborn.

How Much Time

How much time do we have left? To pose such a question is an uncommon reflection in a common world. To step outside of the norm, stand on your pasts shoulders and see your woes clearly and wonder... where have we failed, and where have we been victorious? Looking back- are there any regrets? Are there any outstanding debts? There is an unspoken fear of lost time and melancholy of lost opportunity. It takes a brave heart to pose such a raw question, and the answer, we may never know. The relevancy of time is a construct for our mind- after all, if our past is what was, and our future is what is to come, then the now we create is all we have.

The present. Time exists now and no label we use to pigeon hole its worth may limit its power. The power we all possess only realizing the past doesn't necessarily matter, the future is not yet here and only now is our time.

With that being said, for us uncommon folk in the common world that can be a very lonely thought. Hopes of a future that never comes to pass and a past engulfed in pain that signifies the truth of this thought, there is only now. Right now, is what counts. How much time do we have is <u>not</u> the question. The question is: How much power am I putting forth in the now?

Especially since right now is my past, present and future. The moment I love inside, this thought will become my past memory. It will determine my future, and my presence in it, it will bring me euphoric emotions of blessed joy. I choose an uncommon question to pose in a common word, not how much time- but how bad do you want it _now_?

The question is: How much power am I putting forth in the now? – How Much Time

_____

_____

_____

_____

_____

_____

_____

_____

_____

_____

_____

Do not forget to film a video!

Culture Blog

As the sun's children orbit around their celestial parent, a guiding light leads them. This guiding light burns so bright we can see it from afar. The light I speak of is our sun. Similarly, the founder's purposeful light burns hotter than any other and unifies our solar system, our company. Our beliefs in him to solve a problem whether we are the customer, employee or both we all do believe. It is all encompassing. One ecosystem of shared belief aligns these planets toward their leader, the sun. Entrepreneurship is universal. From the stars and planets, managers to their staff and parents to their children, passion is a guiding light and purpose fuels it. I want to make this truth self-evident; culture is life and all things that matter are manifested from it. It stands to be repeated, culture is life and as an entrepreneur our purpose is to breathe our vision into the people who choose to follow us, so that they may do better for their customer. For the cycle of life goes on. As we let the thought sink in that culture matters in the above-mentioned, we will allow it to grasp our heartstrings and pull on our intellectual cap, but where is the tangibility? Noble leaders ask probing questions and the answer lies in our metaphysical perspective on influence. The individual, who gets to know their followers' story, shares their story and inspires those whom want a new story of what is possible. That defines a leader. This leader is a metaphorical sun in an ecosystem of planets, stars, asteroids and moons. Each solar system is a business, operating around certain inalienable rights, universal principles of truth, gravity, and light speed; the physics of all matter and energy. The sun is the founder of the company or solar system and each planet being an employee. When the suns light radiates bright enough within the perfect distance to its offspring, a planet life is born along with belief and purpose radiating passion. This life is a biosphere capable of producing a microcosm of life itself. These mini earths are only possible due to two factors, purpose and presence. The purpose of the sun to burn bright radiates its passion analogous to the entrepreneur who is so abundant with vision and radiates in energy like a star. With the proper cultivation and oration of this vision his planets align around his gravitational pull. When his vision is clear the possibilities arise for life within his planets, his people. Culture is born, but not quite without the other missing ingredient, presence. Presence is the gravitational pull created by the sheer mass of an object and that object is the size of the leader's vision. His passion radiates so big and his physicality is close enough not to burn the planet but far enough not to freeze his people out. The goal is earth-like, not Mercury or Jupiter. This gravitational pull is coming from the law of leading by showing and not telling. The telling is the passion radiating from alignment with self and comes from purpose, but the equilibrium is formed from also the presence of gravity only birthed through actions and not solely through words. When two ingredients are infused together life forms and that life just so happens to be cultural alignment: A new metaphorical belief system of shared belief between the sun and the earth, the leader and the follower and all due to these inalienable truths; purpose and presence.

Great leaders ask great questions and the answer lies in our metaphysical perspective on leadership. – Culture Blog

_____

_____

_____

_____

_____

_____

_____

_____

_____

_____

_____

_____

Do not forget to film a video!

Refer to page i for directions

Keep reading!
Keep writing!
Keep Filming!

DON'T FORGET TO FILM YOUR VIDEO!

Tag us when you're done!
 Culture Matters
 cultureunitesauthors

#thirtydaysofthought
#culturematters
#readwritespeak
#cultureunitesauthors

What is Consciousness?

Like the holy trinity plus one, there are four horsemen of our internal, eternal and celestial world. These horsemen may rob us of contribution or give to the poor. The answer to what is consciousness lies between these following four. Instinct is fight or flight; feed or fornicate. Emotion lies between stimulus and response. Reason is a choice and letting go is freedom. These four destinations have a trinity of gate keepers of those who work together either enabling or disabling when in fact our consciousness arrives. So, what is consciousness?

Consciousness is the coalition of doing. The road to enlightenment is paved with emotion and our path is carried by our awareness. To do, and not feel is not to live. To feel, and not do is insanity. To think, but not feel is robotic, and to think, do, accept and appreciate is to have it all.

A free state of being is alignment with our maker. The creator of all is our one true self. True self understands peace, love and joy but only through consciousness does upheaval arrive. Consciousness is the holy trinity of thinking, doing, and the state of being. To become aware is to overcome feeling and its unimaginable path to mediocrity. To be aware, present and certain in every moment is the only way to unlock the power of consciousness.

When we understand ourselves and our horsemen, we become Robinhood, and not Musketeers. Consciousness is being on a high level. Being comes from the ability to know how to choose what to do and more importantly, what not to do. Consciousness is freedom, and freedom is the path to awakened understanding, the mirror of truth and our one true self through our reflection. Open the door to consciousness by unveiling yourself to what is right in front of you- the four dimensions, the four horsemen, and the four natures for you to inhabit. They are, instinct, emotion, logic, and letting go, and your answers lie in their awakening. Wake up to your consciousness and lie with yourself in peace as you are what you make of it. Create something of yourself; your life depends on it.

Free state of being is alignment with our maker. The creator of all is our one true self. – What is Consciousness

_____

_____

_____

_____

_____

_____

_____

_____

_____

_____

_____

_____

Do not forget to film a video!

LEAD THROUGH VALUES

We expect others to pick up what we put down. The expectations have been set in stone since the age of industry began. These unalterable and accepted truths are falsely held by the unaware majority. This massive collective of non-leaders but potent managers are hell-bent on diagnosing the miscommunication on their part to the misunderstanding of their pupils. These men, these figure heads of state, tribe and company are sadly mistaken. Chivalry is dead, parenting is not common sense, and management is not what it seems. It must be leadership. To lead is to have another choose by free will to follow. When it comes to leadership leaders are held to the highest standard and values are held higher. Depending on those who follow the values a clear picture of success or failure is painted. When faced with the crossroad between management and leadership, choose the latter; take the promising leap of faith in yourself and the values you hold will impact your people immensely. Lead through purpose, share your heart, wear it on your sleeve, lead from the front and do not tell others what to do without doing it first, model the behavior and more and more people will make the choice to follow. Be the leader that leads from the front.

Lead with purpose, share your heart, wear it on your sleeve, lead from the front and do not tell people what to do, model the behavior and more and more people will make the choice to follow. – Lead Through Values

_____

_____

_____

_____

_____

_____

_____

_____

_____

_____

_____

_____

Do not forget to film a video!

CULTURE DEFINED

Culture is to a society, group, family and species as the lines that pave the way for traffic are to the nearest highway. Culture is a metaphorical ecosystem of shared belief that aligns to a destination. Regardless of whether this destination is positive or negative or right or wrong, these are philosophical questions that may or may not have answers. Culture leads to a destination as any road or highway does a vehicle to any place near or potentially very far away. A shared belief system is sparked by the flame of the influencer. The leader, the foremost alpha specimen of the pack, and the king of the universe among all men and women is who we choose to follow. Dependent on oration ability and strength whether physical or mental we follow this leader in our journey starting with a single step. If we agree to form a definition around culture being a metaphorical ecosystem of shared belief created by an influencer and maintained by the alignment of the influenced, then what does this mean? Why is it vital to study, codify and harness a concise understanding of culture to develop a company to its highest echelon of performance? The answers to these questions are simple, life as we know it is a product of our environment, whether we give the credit to natural selection and Darwin or to a deity ever so high up in the clouds, we are here, we are present, and our thoughts are to create. The thoughts we think create visions and these visions spark actions which lead to a process. The process of thought to action to outcome trickles into stackable results that lead to change. A person's culture or internal metaphorical ecosystem creates matter, or their material results as does infinite creator or whomever credit we choose to give life. People aspire to higher purpose which is defined as self-actualization. Self-actualization is in its hierarchy of basic essential needs for a person to create meaning in life. Most hunger is satiated, most safety is attained, most esteem is observed, and love is mostly felt even if it is just for a moment. We will be doomed to forever darkness without purpose, self-actualization and self-awareness. We mostly never take the time to search or pursue the journey of self-introspection and we mostly never care deeply enough to learn of what "we don't know, we don't know." What could be a prominent and pragmatic solution? Well, since work takes up 25-50% of our lives subtracted by sleep, play and self-gratification, we will only pursue due to lack of self-actualization to begin with. If a company is the product of one influencer who has a vision to a solution of a problem then it only makes perfect spiritual, logical and emotional sense for that being to lay out their inner self-actualization or purpose in clear and concise context for their followers, peers and people to rise too. Most may never find their answers within their hearts for whatever reason, but that does not stop the founder, the leader and the influencers from laying out a foundation of values. Like the saints of older ages or dogmatic dictations, the values, commandments, rules and regulations of living so many hundreds of millions speak of, live by, and hold true to can be modeled by our leaders in business. After all, by forming an agreement with a new definition of business that is founded on the vision then all other details and systems are but mere effects of the cause; the solution. If a business achieves that then it is as important and may be as empowering as countless religions, faiths, and spiritual journeys one may ever travel upon. A future of abundance, love, grace and humanity starts with the company first. Their adjustment to their vision, mission, purpose and values are the catalyst. A happy workplace leads to a happy spouse or partner, and a happy spouse or partner leads to a happy home, a happy home to happy off spring, happy offspring to a happy family, community, city, state, nation, country, continent, world, earth and a global civilization founded on one common collective; human culture matters.

We will be doomed to forever darkness without purpose, self-actualization and self-awareness. – Culture Defined

_____

_____

_____

_____

_____

_____

_____

_____

_____

_____

_____

_____

Do not forget to film a video!

Refer to page i for directions

Keep reading!
Keep writing!
Keep Filming!

DON'T FORGET TO FILM YOUR VIDEO!

Tag us when you're done!
Culture Matters
cultureunitesauthors

#thirtydaysofthought
#culturematters
#readwritespeak
#cultureunitesauthors

WT-Matrix
(Word Thought – Matrix)

No thought is wasted nor word un-done. Belief understood to the depths of possibility or influence wasted as our universe is much too churlish for that. With every utterance evoked from within our shared self of our collective unconscious is untouchable, disprovable, and yet indescribably more valid than comprehension. Our mind may not be definable but sleeps wakes and resides amongst us due to a very metaphysical fact; we must heed warning that all energy in this universe is forever and among that energy are our truths. These stories we tell ourselves and shared amongst those imposing on our reality. Every word, thought, idea, belief and conviction created may never be destroyed. Surely it will go on forever, the pebble splashing the pond of life or a yawn in a sea of tired persons. Our energy is never lost as it is only found by another space in time and another construct of mind. This mind or our self within itself creates powerless labels to our own realizations stuck in a mashed picture, inside the frame and trapped from all answers lost within ourselves. Recognize this power inside you, inside us and freedom may join you. The potential of freedom tracking along this journey becomes possible with awareness alone. The recognition is that this matrix, word-thought, idea and behavior cycle is perpetual living and thus surreal. It is around us, inside us and it is us. Whatever we can conclude "us" to be, we are this WT-Matrix so learning how it works, and the power/energy hold in our lives is the key to unlock your life's metaphorical safe. The safe is where important answers are kept. The safe is where the truths you may need to hear with all five senses for you to transform, transfer and come into yourself; full transcendence. This is WT-Matrix!

Our energy is never lost as it is only found by another space in time
and another construct of the mind. – WT-Matrix

_____

_____

_____

_____

_____

_____

_____

_____

_____

_____

_____

Do not forget to film a video!

O +/- M = B

All desired outcomes are and must be measured against ones pre-conceived matrix or notion of current reality; this is represented by the letter, "M." Through the looking glass of life all that is seen, and unseen is a determinate of this said matrix. Your preconceived matrix or reality is the current accumulation of biases up to the ripe old age of your current self. These are your stackable lenses covering your metaphorical eye glasses that may never come off and may never be recognized until now. When an outcome of any nature is weighed against our current matrix there is a result. This result effects is our new-found belief (B). Dependent upon the energy force whether positive or negative of the outcome and the current force energy of your thought matrix in respect to the discipline, the belief will be lesser or greater or negative or positive. All newfangled realities in consciousness can be broken down by this formula O (+ or -) M=B the outcome of any behavior be it positive or negative weighed against the current preconceived matrix with a new energy force; belief (B) in the context of the behavior rendered and conscious perspective resulting. Whether the subject matter is positive, or negative is relevant in respect to our matrix. Our matrix holds the key to whether we have enough positive or negative current of energy to determine the belief system appropriately. Based on our current (+ or -) (M), we may or may not overcome negative or positive stimulus. In the respect to the latter, we also figure out that we may or may not need mentorship in respect to the current discipline in front of us. We always need some type of mentorship. This equation is funda-mental in understanding limiting beliefs or self as well as establishing leadership amongst cognitive controlled organisms or followers. Are you in control of your reality?

O +/- M = B

(Outcome or Stimulus) (+/-) (Current Matrix) = (Belief)

Read the following excerpt as a pair

Formula I: Sa +/- M = Oa +/- M = Ba
Formula II: Ba +/- M = Ma

Formula I Example: -10 + 15 = 5 + 15 = 20
Formula II Example: 20 + 15 = 35

Formula I Example Continued: -10 + 35 = 25 + 35 = 60
Formula II Example Continued: 60 +35 = 95

Formula I Example: -10 - 15 = -25 - 15 = -40
Formula II Example: -40 - 15 = -55

Formula I Example Continued: -10 - 55 = -65 - 55 = -120
Formula II Example Continued: -120 - 55 = -175

(Ma) It is the specificity of our singular beliefs that influence our individual matrix which stacks on top of itself creating our average positive or negative character represented as (M).

(a) represents the object or context under the subjective conflict of an individual's (M).

(M) or Matrix represents an individual's average energy field whether positive or negative.

(Sa) represents stimulus in context of perception from an individual's (M).

(Oa) represents the outcomes energy, positive or negative based on

(Sa) juxtaposed by an individual's (M).

(Ba) Belief is an individual's quantitative prescription of their lens in reference to a specific context.

It represents the positive or negative added or subtracted to ones preconceived matrix in relation to (a) or the observed and translates to a schema.

"It is our evolution that brings us internal resolution."

The Formula
Formula I: Sa +/- M = Oa +/- M = Ba
Formula II: Ba +/- M = Ma

"Change the way you look at things and the things you look at change." – Wayne Dyer

It was through the lens of a surface level edit that an at bottom dissection took place, a check-up, turned brain scan, turned lobotomy. In the moment upon realization, my matrix was shaken by negative (S), or stimulus. The realization I could improve within the fear of failure and a timeline not met was against my current matrix of reality be it positive or negative overall and that would be measured as outcome (O). This outcome can be positive or negative and that is the proof of (Oa +/- M = Ba), belief in the respective object, situation or occurrent energy in alignment with anyone's matrix. This end result or positive or negative (Ba) added or deducted to the average matrix of reality creates an overall average expression of being either positive or negative. An example being the top baseball player who is confident in their ability to play cricket (a similar game) as their confidence is positive or negative equals (M) (e.g. Michael Jordan playing baseball was due to exponential conflation of his individual M without equality of necessary utility). The baseball experiences resulted in belief structures, (Ba), with (a) symbolizing baseball as context, and their

(M) equates to the overall matrix or reality. These belief structures are the result of compounded (Ba) plus a series of (M) sets acted out over time which led to the cross belief in cricket due to causality of increased (M). This is where Formula II comes in, (Ba +/- M = Ma). (Ma) represents the perception of (Sa) in relation to an individual's (M), (Ma) is their competence in respect to a specific context. It is the series of (Ma) sets that increase confidence in other fields like the previously cited examples. This is competence and confidence cycled to make up their thoughts, words, ideals, beliefs, habits and results as an average (M). The (Sa) or stimulus that was faced in baseball filtered through their (M) equated to the outcome (O). This outcome is weighed against the (M) and leads to (Ba) which equals a higher chance the baseball player has confidence in the game of cricket. For example, in the moment of truth at negative 50(S), a decision is made at positive 51(M), and the outcome is positive one with a result that will be added or deducted to the preconceived positive or negative (M). Furthermore, (Ba) or belief equating to positive or negative is weighed against said activity (-50(Sa) + 51(M)= 1(Oa) + 51(M) = 52(Ba), 52(Ba) + 51(M) = 103(Ma)). The more positive (Ba) in context, the more likely (Sa) is easy to overcome in the future represented as (Ma). We continue to gain energy with every step forward and every overcoming of said stimulus or (Sa). The stimulus is a mirage and it is our matrix or stacked energy perception that results in our behaviors resulting in the outcomes. At this point, the gradient is not available, but the concept and philosophy are clear! Choose to detach negative emotion from (Sa) and focus on micro wins. For the (O) will be positive plus your (M) resulting in a higher (Ba) and leading to a greater (Ma) thus increasing your average (M). Your atomic power will surge and no situation (Sa), stimulus (Sa) or person (Sa), will slow your progress down.

Remember: Sa +/- M = Oa +/- M = Ba and Ba +/- M = Ma, and repeat...

The Lesson for The Formula

The two excerpts above are representatives for us today and show us who we are, the parent and the offspring. The first a work in progress and the second still under the pressure of overcoming. Your author would beg the difference of the two as a more refined distillation of an abstract concept of speech that plagues their mind day and night. The goal is to create a gradient to measure energy transference between man leading to expression of oneself in a more atomic way. Although we are not quite there yet, progress is in order and this metaphor summarizes your book, what you hold in your hands this moment and what you currently read right now as a tool for evolution. This is a growth of an idea; a theory. Neither of our jobs are done as of yet, so we will both keep on keeping on, read to think, write to develop, listen to understand and speak to let go. All in all, it is our evolution that brings us internal resolution, our Thirty Days of Thought.

- The **matrix** represents our average current energy field or internal belief construct that is the make-up of our character. (M)
- The **belief** represents in the equation a positive or negative matrix relative to the contextual subject matter observation. E.g.: H.O.T. Call, presentation, speech, argument, discipline or debate. (B)
- The **outcome** and the **stimulus** represent initial stimulus collocated by an average matrix and the outcome of that energy equation. (OS)
- The **matrix in a specific context** is the result of Formula I and Formula II. (Ma)

Disclaimer: Up to this point we can only infer that if one's (Ma) or Matrix in a specific context increases or decreases, their (M) will increase or decrease, but not until a gradient is created and testing is done can we prove or disprove this theory. Currently, using Maslow's hierarchy and other psychological theories, we can infer when one's (Ma) increases there is an opportunity for them to climb higher into love and belonging by usefully adding value both materially and immaterially to themselves through others. This perpetual spiral upward in utility creates more meaning and actualized behavior while increasing confidence. This does not necessarily attribute itself to self-awareness and intrapsychic development over trauma but does increase independence in correlating success in one area to perceived success in others. Therefore, gaining competence in one context increases one's (Ma) or Matrix in a specific context. This is believed to have spill-over in other fields and in the individual's overall reality or individuality represented as their (M) or matrix.

Read to think, write to develop, listen to understand and speak to let go. – The Lesson

_____

_____

_____

_____

_____

_____

_____

_____

_____

_____

_____

Do not forget to film a video!

CONNECTED

The circle is formed, and a breath is unanimously inhaled and exhaled; we are one. The covenant, group, and culture of bodies is all decided upon one truth; a united stance for the same thing. For without hesitation or fear the causes that lifts people up grant them power over their adversities. Whomever the foe may be today they are in no way of harm, whatever obstacle may fall in their path, it will never slow them down, and whatever fate challenges their faith, the conviction they hold together will never waiver. These men, women and their children are connected. This connection of collective consciousness aligns their behavior and manifests all indefinite results. Without oneness they are lost, after all, what else could be the purpose of life but to work together? Although glittered with irony, when we team up it allows us to identify our individual strengths with an innate ability to contribute to other people's weaknesses, so we exponentially improve all together. Cultural alignment is the bridge to this connected cause. There is no other imagined hypothesis that can undermine this for this represents the meaning of life that is brought unto us by us and for us. Therefore, we need us. We yearn for something greater than ourselves, we are selfishly selfless, and it is our psychological altruism that is guided by our biological selfish genes; these are the precursors to pass on the codes of life. Love, faith, trust, anger, and desire are all intertwined in the template of design of our label of life. Upon multiple studies, it is evident our fate is destined to connectivity. The question posed is, how? Will we interlock hands and praise one another for our labors of love, kindness and joy, or will we cross swords and demand respect with fear, harm and strength. Whether we consciously realize these truths or not they are imbedded within. The codes of our selfish genes are preset as they are passed on from the outcomes of our struggle, the fights of our ancestors and the flights of their survival. This road map has been graphed prior to our birth and laid down before us but how the story unravels is thrust upon us by our will. We are connected and together we can achieve success. We feel right aiding each other and abiding by these moralistic laws set forth by our leaders. It is in our nature to love, prosper and be one with each other. The connectivity of our nature is all we can count on to save us and give us meaning far beyond the here and the now. Connectivity guarantees our present life and continues our future by providing us offspring. How we connect is up to us, laid down by our biology but executed on by our psychology. Be you, be free, and choose good for evil is just as easy but not as beautiful or connected.

The connectivity of our nature is all we can count on to save us and give us meaning far beyond the here and the now. – Connected

_____

_____

_____

_____

_____

_____

_____

_____

_____

_____

_____

_____

_____

Do not forget to film a video!

Refer to page i for directions

Keep reading!
Keep writing!
Keep Filming!

DON'T FORGET TO FILM YOUR VIDEO!

Tag us when you're done!
Culture Matters
cultureunitesauthors

#thirtydaysofthought
#culturematters
#readwritespeak
#cultureunitesauthors

GOALS

It wasn't that she aimed so high and missed, it was that she aimed low enough just to hit. A sound goal in mind is what she had been conditioned to think necessary to succeed. Actions are necessary to manifest results of any kind, but we set the bar of life so low that we fail to realize the types of goals we need to set. Goals hold no internal meaning but a false ideology we place on them. Unless our goals reflect our soul, they will hold no charm to our hearts. Our hearts will not beat for them and without a heartbeat there is no pulse, and without a pulse the person is dead and so is the goal. Goals come from the perspective of purpose. No, it was not that she aimed too high or just low enough, it was that her goal was not riddled with flame. A burning desire from within emanating from her being proposing a new idea, a calling so profound that her mind had no limit and zero doubt could be formed. There is no fear, there is no pain and there is no judgment- only certainty of what is and why it is. That is a goal, the reassured confidence that what must be done gets done and no one or nothing can stop her. That is a goal, and that goal is rooted in purpose, birthed from within and the reflection of one's soul that anything became possible. She aimed higher and she hit harder. In this new-found perception she found her goals and they were a reflection of her being. Her potential became her goals and her goals were infinite.

"Actions are necessary to manifest results of any kind, but we set the bar of life so low that we fail to realize the types of goals we need to set." - Goals

_____

_____

_____

_____

_____

_____

_____

_____

_____

_____

_____

_____

Do not forget to film a video!

TRAJECTORY

Cast away from the masses as the lone wolf embarks on a journey glittered with allure and objects representing instant gratification. These shrines are painted in gold that lead to wandering eyes, hollow hearts and empty minds. In a zombie-like state of being un-enthralled by the beauties of life and contentious toward others whom seem at bliss; everyone else. This journey of success is a difficult one. It is a lonely one. This journey is not for the faint of heart, and it surely is not for those who just want the simple satisfactions. If one is not clear on who they are, what they want and why they fight their trajectory can lead them down a devilish path, not of love, but of hatred, not of courage, but of pride, not of acceptance, but of indifference. Trajectory is going over and going under; trajectory is the catalyst of the humble man or the man of righteous endeavor-the man who does as he says, a man that does not waver. This man is on a trajectory to his highest self. At our journeys end and our journeys beginning two forks shape themselves as effects to the cause of striving. These forks are that of tragedies or trajectories, without choosing you will travel one. Choose to be who you are and do not decide who you are not. Stay on the trajectory of self, be you, be your greatest self.

At our journeys end and our journeys beginning two forks shape themselves as effects to the cause of striving. – Trajectory

_____

_____

_____

_____

_____

_____

_____

_____

_____

_____

_____

Do not forget to film a video!

Saying No to the Homeless

People lie to the homeless or even worse they give, selfishly! They must stop this immediately on behalf of both parties involved. This is the way for our human race, our social, spiritual and rational being to degenerate itself, wholly and into infinitude. I hear you squabble amongst yourselves, my readers belittling my thought, and at that, I will persist due to love and acceptance. For these words are for our future together. I know your truth is rattled and intuition tells you sound advice as per usual, but not in this case I dare declare! For that I beg of your adherence to a hypothetical view of an imaginative representation of another world; the world of honesty and non-omission. A world founded in truth, your truth. Hence the former statement indubitably stated in loving embrace, that of indefinitely saying no to the homeless or beggars. These beggars of which appear in need and pull on yours and my heart-strings. Ah, for in that thought there lies an actual hell, that of reality and functionality in motion. After all, what do we do? Morally, ethically, and virtuously, what do we do? To give without a new path set forth is perpetual damnation and a continual catalyst for these people, humans, mothers, sons, daughters, brothers, sisters, homeless and beggars to stay in the same state they are already in. These homeless given bread or coin in fear of being rude, condemns unconscious wrath upon them or appears non-socially accepted in a meek and humble world is only a lie to yourself. You lie to yourself daily as you deviate from, "no," as you delineate your lies in subtle omissions of, "I'm sorry I do not have cash," as if you would hand it over in due course if you did! And if it is done, how so? Courage? Neutrality? I deem that not the case. You are in fear and suffer from awkward guilt. I know this to be true because I am you, a red devil, human I am, all too human, for I know this to be our truth. And in all these meager retorts of nonsense justifications to betray your love by omitting and lying, you devalue one important person, yourself.

Keep saying yes and overtime you yourself will sink into the filth of it; the muck of lies you tell them and yourself. Overtime your self-love will dwindle and fear will build, inconsistency will prevail, and intrinsic value will deteriorate. Each time a lie utters henceforth your lips that you can be, the potential inside of you dwindles in forever perpetuation and nothing done can be undone in due course. For that I beg of you, wake up and help yourself help this man or woman of homelessness. For with two beggars, one for money or food and one for a social contract deemed worthy, that of you, all will indefinitely be lost. For if both parties fall in deep enough waters and neither with the ability to swim everyone will be doomed to suffer the same outcome, death. As I digress into my cave safely at ease from the outburst of hell and damnation cast my way, after such an essay regardless of my intent, I leave you with questions unperturbed by ill emotion, but only rooted in love and a greater ideal. Questions bore out of experience for the cause justly stated prior to. Love in my heart and courage in this transcription I leave you with this ... Want to change their fate? Ask them their name...Want to give? Listen to them... Want to show love to another? Bestow inspiration with your story and a hug in momentary silence while staying authentic and embracing your new reflection of soul; the homeless. Say no to their nature and yes to your higher being so you both may become better. For without the latter their matter of circumstance will not change, and you will not matter to yourself. Omitting, lying, avoiding and devouring yourself intrinsically with anything other than truth are the absolute death of spirit, mind and soul and that would be saying anything other than the word, "no!" The truth is, "no," and you know it, hence the more you hate me in this moment upon reading my piece- I still love you. Therefore, just like you and the homeless, I will not let your nature subdue our potential greater being. I will always tell the truth. Alas, if you, my reader, are in fact a saint, keep giving because that is the fate you have chosen and chosen well.

Each time a lie utters henceforth your lips that you can be, the potential inside of you dwindles in forever perpetuation and nothing done can be undone in due course. – Saying No to the Homeless

_____

_____

_____

_____

_____

_____

_____

_____

_____

_____

_____

_____

Do not forget to film a video!

THE MORE YOU TEACH, THE HIGHER YOUR POTENTIAL

Stacked on top of each other one by one, each thought more profound than the last. This stacking is the result of a big heart, a sound mind and intent to share, with every idea demonstrated through an immense feeling to enable another to grow; the teacher becomes the student. Studious in thought but compounded by their brains medicinal way of developing new ideas. The genius in natures plan lies in the biological mechanisms of the mind. Our anthropologic design to intuit our shared thoughts and strive to philosophize against them is to grapple with what we know now and create what we will agree to know next. If we want to unlock our minds ceiling and unhinge its symbolic gates of limitation, we must let go and share. True wisdom is the knowledge that all thoughts are not necessarily our own but borrowed energy that enables action and commands reaction. It is only in our ability to share that we may ever tap into our unknown potential. This is our destined fate. Teaching is our biological calling and to disown it or fight against its burden will be our reckoning. When our intellectual, ontological and spiritual grips tighten we hold back thus saving our knowledge to ourselves. This is the path to limitation in that without cognition we enact it daily by resisting the urge to share. When we become aware of the truth regarding competition being a myth then our hope of the infinite becomes possible. After all, the more you teach the higher your potential. Potential love, potential understanding and potential action will come from within, but *only* after sharing because natural selection is very selective, and it is up to you to decide. Keep sharing your way to your highest potential.

True wisdom is the knowledge that all thoughts are not necessarily our own but borrowed energy that enables action and commands reaction. - The More You Teach, The Higher Your Potential

_____

_____

_____

_____

_____

_____

_____

_____

_____

_____

_____

_____

Do not forget to film a video!

Refer to page i for directions

Keep reading!
Keep writing!
Keep Filming!

DON'T FORGET TO
FILM YOUR VIDEO!

Tag us when you're done!
 Culture Matters
 cultureunitesauthors

#thirtydaysofthought
#culturematters
#readwritespeak
#cultureunitesauthors

Mentee

Listen to understand not to reply. Be open as if you are a cup awaiting its next pour of aqua. The life force of our cups usefulness for the consumer is hinged on the cups ability to let go, be free from constraint and unfastened from its lid. As the cup is to its pourer and as the cup is to its consumer, we must be open to our mentor and useful to our mentee. Life has a cycle and to break it is to defy life itself. In that betrayal we are evil. In that misalignment lays contradiction to the laws of nature. This expression of defiance is what we call arrogance and this act is stemmed from a broken cup. Broken in a sense of what lies beneath the surface, below the ice burgs tip in the bowels of its soul. A void endlessly doubting, closed off, manipulating the pourer and consumers, the mentor and the mentee. This betrayal of the cycle is blasphemy and this betrayal means death. Life cannot go on for we are broken, we are closed, and the lid is sealed tight. Our one true oath must matter, law recyclability- Our responsibility to be a cup capable of pouring into another receiving, accepting and sharing what we learned. Our essence is necessary if this cycle is the essence of life itself. Properly demonstrated in all fundamental relationships, the crux of the cosmic dance of star to earth or the expression of parent to offspring, this mentor correspondence is our cup of life therefore, drink and pour- openly.

Dedicated to the future generations

"Our essence is necessary if this cycle is the essence of life itself.
– Mentee

_____

_____

_____

_____

_____

_____

_____

_____

_____

_____

_____

_____

Do not forget to film a video!

Success is Love

Success is not found; it is the freedom of choice. Success is a decision to choose your every thought, word and action. Success is not something to reach for, but a state of being that overtime can be cultivated by the journey of life. The pendulum swings of hardship, achievement, anger and love. As I write this that feeling of euphoria reverberating through my every inch is success. This feeling is organic. My feelings in this moment are real and present. Please open yourself and hear me, my friend. Success is who you are and who you become in the process. True success can only be described in one word. The word is not a noun, but a verb. The word you know well, it describes the first moment you were birthed and looked up at Mom; it's love. Success is one state, love. Choose love.

Date _____

Success is who you are and who you become in the process. - Success Is Love

_____

_____

_____

_____

_____

_____

_____

_____

_____

_____

_____

_____

Do not forget to film a video!

OUR ARRIVAL

Every so often we are blessed to have arrived. Our bags have been packed or will be in a hurry, a clocks tick has sounded, an alarm sounding a necessary decision. As our blood flows through each vein and every hair follicle stands on end, the time we've been waiting for has presented itself; the opportunity of a life time. As I write this, I feel aligned with this moment. My mind, heart and soul are one. My friends, the family I have chosen are those whom I feel one with. The business we have built has been pieced together through passion alone, and the time has come to reap what we have sown. When life throws you curve balls and you're on your back there's nowhere else to look but up. Knowing that those whom you've struggled with are lying next to you always does and will give you the inner strength to pull through. After all, pulling yourself off the ground from your boot straps is easy when you have a nearby shoulder to lean on. In this moment I reminisce in times that were contrary to my current alignment, times filled with pain, and not fulfillment. Although things were hard, I cannot regret, but only gratefully acknowledge the choices made and who I became throughout it all. The hours that slowly crept by and feelings that seemed to linger, lonely thoughts reverberating through my consciousness repeating the negative disclaimer, "turn back, give up." As I decide right now in this moment to take the leap and move forward with my team I think back to those moments- awkward and lonely beginnings that forged this sword of comradeship. It is only now that we may swing together and cut through any obstacles that may have been sliced through before. Only now we are not alone. We have arrived.

My friends, the family I have chosen are those whom I feel one with.
– Our Arrival

_____

_____

_____

_____

_____

_____

_____

_____

_____

_____

_____

Do not forget to film a video!

Refer to page i for directions

Keep reading!
Keep writing!
Keep Filming!

DON'T FORGET TO FILM YOUR VIDEO!

Tag us when you're done!

f Culture Matters

📷 cultureunitesauthors

#thirtydaysofthought
#culturematters
#readwritespeak
#cultureunitesauthors

TRUTH

Truth lies in the eye of the beholder and to each their own in the reality of what is and what isn't. Fundamental truths empirically stated beyond any rational doubt does neither party any good if one party refuses to be wrong. And it is not the truest of the match that wins the argument, but only the doer willing and able to do more to defend their truth. With this observation comes a universal truth that reality is subjective and even with underlying truths cementing us all together in this game called life we can and will bring contradictory meaning to our shared experience. These unwavering, personal, cultural, societal, political, ideological fragmented truths can and will undermine whatever invisible or intrinsic truths do exist. Due to the unfortunate truth of the previous statement, our truest truths may never be found. If this is true in its very nature, what future can we possibly create but a limited reality of fragmented social, cultural structures all fighting for an opportunity to be right? What if the question of truth alone was the issue? That the only pragmatic truth is that there is no necessary truth and that truth of truth lies. That the only absolute truth is that there is not truth, but the truth that there is no truth, but temporary utility backed up by meaning. Truth itself is a contradiction and proves to be a lie. Dare I say it here that truth is dead, and the very belief in truth contradicts truth because it undermines another truth interpreting that the only truth, we have is that we are all a cosmic lie. Stuck on truth is the arrogant organism lying to himself; the human.

It is not the truest of the match that wins the argument, but only the doer willing and able to do more to defend their truth. With this observation comes a universal truth that reality is subjective and even with underlying truths cementing us all together in this game called life we can and will bring contradictory meaning to our shared experience. - Truth

_____

_____

_____

_____

_____

_____

_____

_____

_____

_____

_____

_____

Do not forget to film a video!

REFLECT AND RELEASE

In times of stress you wonder, or we wonder. The wonder leads to wisdom, but the wondering will always end in ignorance. In the shadow of the unknown lives the man with no face, no identity, and no comprehension of worth. The only outcome of the wonderer is malevolence of thy self. An introverted appearance the longing for something more and a bitter sweet comprehension of anything better, this one thing close enough to imagine but too far seeing. Without sight he cannot find what cannot be found and what will never exist. There he is… a wonderer lost in his own head, the caged mind of an individual left to his own devices. A man who does not know what he does not know that he is but a wonderer. But then with a flash of brilliance change occurs. Something or someone crosses his path be it a book, experience, possibility or a guide. This new piece in his puzzle of life gives opportunity to our wonderer beyond his wildest dreams. The opportunity to reflect, think and in turn comprehend. With comprehension comes knowing and to know is to release. Release the burden of ignorance and the pain in fear. All weights of ignorance burning down on this wonderer starts to glide off his shoulders, the smug looks of competition fall off as their visualizations are perturbed by a new posture this man exudes. His shoulder is back, chin is up, and arms are outstretched. This man's new reality is that of the awakened; a free man in a slave world. A being of faith, and trust in himself so he may trust his common man this wonderer has become oh wise one man of reflection, a man of release. Upon visual perception we see a new man staring back at us in the mirror of life, but his outward appearance only shows a tip of an iceberg of inner strength. This man of wisdom is but a volcano waiting to burst and tread into the heart of the core. His earth, his maker, his master this wonderer has transformed through one thing and one thing alone, reflection.... What can we draw from man? To live a life free, a life of meaning and inner strength we must reflect upon our every moment, so we may release the burdens of life. The follower wonders after the wonderer who knows enough to create meaning; therefore, the wonderer becomes wise enough to lead. This is our responsibility as man, as woman, as a being of comprehension, as the individual with two faces wise or wonder, who will you be?

With comprehension comes knowing and to know is to release. –
Reflect and Release

_____

_____

_____

_____

_____

_____

_____

_____

_____

_____

_____

_____

_____

Do not forget to film a video!

HAPPY BIRTHDAY

A socially acceptable reoccurrence of time and an observation of matter filled with dreams for those moments' past; this is the birthday of old. A time inspired for those who have just begun life's journey; this is the birthday of young. To look back on a year of happenings poses an important perspective shift: is the glass half full or glass half empty? Do we need the labels of material observation such as age to define our life's value unto others? Would such a thing as defining ones constructed time on this earth be of value in the grand scheme of things? How can we propel ourselves further without holding ourselves back when we limit our abilities due to something unreal, untrue, and only upheld through ignorance? Our age... I dare demand this to stop! The material observation and enslavement by an unconscious axiom holds truth to timeliness, but not due to causality. This is not due to our age, but our efforts! The causality of choice, the urge of exploration, the wisdom due to curiosity and the grit developed through sacrifice not by length of time involved in the game of life. Happy birthday to you, the reader. For as you digest this blurb of tumultuous and thoughtful provocation you stand to differ from the masses. You are now potentially aware of these unknown ignorance's of the ridiculousness of my enemy and now yours, age. The celebration of nothing more than a clock ticking, and a noise beating in our eardrum is nothing of value. No man or woman has done unto others any greater due to a number we choose to define ourselves by. The men, women and children that have devastated the world and dug up the diamonds within themselves did so without second thought, without questioning such things as age and did so without hesitation. These overmen were tried, true and riddled with thoughts of complexity to abstract for a number to define. A number we call, age. What is 20? What is 30? What is 80? Ignorance itself lies in the lies we tell ourselves, agreeable to this social construction called age. For in a moment of wisdom we need not label our genius, but to the contrary we will stand tall by our virtues and execute on them with our word and with our actions! Hear me! Age is just a number, a birthday is a mere revelation of possibility, and we should be celebrating what occurs every day that of utter brilliance called life. With a glass half full and genius interpretation of reality, we are all conquerors of ourselves and our birthday is every day. With that my friends, my enemies, and my collaborators- Celebrate your life right now by being a force for good, for truth and that of wisdom. Think about it. Happy birthday today, and to you.

Nothing of value comes from such observations as age, young nor old. – Happy Birthday

_____

_____

_____

_____

_____

_____

_____

_____

_____

_____

_____

_____

Do not forget to film a video!

Refer to page i for directions

Keep reading!
Keep writing!
Keep Filming!

DON'T FORGET TO FILM YOUR VIDEO!

Tag us when you're done!
f Culture Matters
⊙ cultureunitesauthors

#thirtydaysofthought
#culturematters
#readwritespeak
#cultureunitesauthors

TALK

Everyone has a story. You see, we are not so different. For the same reasons, we push those who are not us away one could surmise that we pull them close. We all share some things universally and you may ask what they are...first and foremost, humanity. After that, we share the following but are not limited to pain, fear, shame, pride, hope, lust, guilt, apathy, love, desire, and the list goes on. As we search our mind the soul is what we carry as a burden and not as a gift. The amalgamation of emotion spreads through our cognition tainting our worth and dividing ourselves. This is what we call our, "story," and we use our stories to cut ties or connect them to one another. What do I say to this truth, fact, fallacy, detriment or malevolence? I say, TALK, for it is our only solution. There could never be such a detrimental and diabolical label as the label of a stranger. This pre-historic word left unto us during infancy and beyond to protect us from those we do not know. Our ancestors, our blood, our mothers, and our fathers were given these prerequisites to share with us. They deserve the credit for our consciousness being that they served us first; however, they and we need strangers. We are modern, forthright, loving, rational, aware, actualized, and in control of our better or worse nature, and therefore we do not need to use the antique term such as, "stranger" anymore. Do unto others as you would have them do unto yourself and talk to strangers. Human culture matters and needs no strangers. Do not be afraid to talk to strangers as everyone has a story. It is their story, your story and our story that separates or qualifies us and that will remain a choice forever. The choice is always up to you, so talk.

Dedicated to Antoinette for creating our company value, Talk!

Do not be afraid to talk to strangers as everyone has a story. It is their story, your story and our story that separates or qualifies us and that will remain a choice forever. – Talk

_____

_____

_____

_____

_____

_____

_____

_____

_____

_____

_____

_____

Do not forget to film a video!

THE GREATEST DECEPTION MEN SUFFER IS FROM THEIR OWN OPINION

The canyon of knowing is as wide as it must be, to be unrecognized to the naked eye and deeper than cognition as it may pick up its shadow of malevolence. The evil in men is born in their surety of mind especially when tossing with a counterpart's truth. That of man and woman, masculine and feminine is juxtaposed as equally wrong in knowing absolutes. All that is well known to men is birthed within the canyon of clear sight and assured presumption. The battles over kin, the wars over land and spiritual dogmas the offspring of man's greatest deception are only his love for his own opinion. The shroud of purest reason like an invisible albatross weighing down the enlightenment of the individual whilst man is deceived by his own view, the sight of truth cannot be seen, and he is doomed to the purgatory of being right. Our human condition of greatness is caged by its own deception that of the truest and most absolute opinion. And all whom surround man's passing are at the woes of his reason.

Dedicated to Leonardo da Vinci

Men's greatness is caged by his own deception that of his truest opinion. – The Greatest Deception Men Suffer is From Their Own Opinion

_____

_____

_____

_____

_____

_____

_____

_____

_____

_____

_____

_____

_____

Do not forget to film a video!

BE THE WAVE

Once the tides of perspectives are raised, they cannot fall back to their origins. What side of the Tsunami are you on?

Each incident or occurrence and every story told unto self brings us closer to the storm. Odds are we are stuck in it, but the question is which side are we facing? We can either sail our wave to the shore line of our hope, of our dearest future or we can drown in our own sorrows. With life its simple, things happen, the question that must be raised is not whether these happenings were right or wrong. The true myths we must search through are within us and it starts with our perspective. Did this wave hit us out of love or harm? Harm is the sense of happening to us and love is the reality for us, for boundless expansion and growth. No matter what we are in an eternal tangle with life's tsunami, we must knowingly understand and decide which way we are facing. How can we take control and ride these waves of perspective? Simple, we choose a laugh not a sneer, a smile against a frown and a hug versus a push. Every act acted upon or against all occurrences or happenings are opportunities. Waves of perspective wash over us with each tide. They cleanse our sins or kill our own wins. Life is but a tsunami, part of the eternal ecosystem. We decide what role we will play in the universal dance. Once the tides of perspectives are raised there is no going back to their origin, only hell awaits the individual drowning to their peril dying to be the effect to life's tsunami. Be great, be your life's change, be the wave.

Every act acted upon or against all occurrences or happenings are opportunities. – Be the Wave

_____

_____

_____

_____

_____

_____

_____

_____

_____

_____

_____

Do not forget to film a video!

Refer to page i for directions

Keep reading!
Keep writing!
Keep Filming!

DON'T FORGET TO FILM YOUR VIDEO!

Tag us when you're done!
 Culture Matters
 cultureunitesauthors

#thirtydaysofthought
#culturematters
#readwritespeak
#cultureunitesauthors

Word – Title of Our Life

Every word we utter, every word we preach is a container of possibility, the infinite possibility of creation. If we think back to our thought, we can remember the action inspired directly from it this is due to our devotion to our nature. Thoughts are here for us, with us and they are us. Words are our thoughts metaphorical keepers, the words we speak keep in line the energy of our thoughts and they influence those near us and those apart from us. The words we speak, transcribe and leave behind long after we are gone reverberate throughout time bouncing off others and instilling wisdom in the few who listen to understand. When it comes to the word we tend to think lightly and that is why life can be so dark. We find ourselves stuck in conflict plagued by the unaware repercussions of the word, the ripple effect of past negative energy bouncing back to us knocking us in the face. Although, before we get hit there is something we can do. We can think twice before we speak. Watch yourself and be wary of your word for each utterance may signify the beginning of creation or death to an extent. When surrounded by your friends treat them with care, and when surrounded by your enemies, be wise as the words you share could be your last. Around your profession, speak up and warrant respect. When you find yourself with a mate be clear- communication is key as that is where alignment is created. In public, be calm as only those amongst followers lose their cool regardless of circumstance whether positive or negative. Each word you share holds a meaning so speak clearly and with conviction. Own your word and own your story for life is a book and each word create a title; the story of the book reflects its title.

Watch yourself and be wary of your word for each utterance may signify the beginning of creation or death to an extent. – Word – Title of Our Life

_____

_____

_____

_____

_____

_____

_____

_____

_____

_____

_____

_____

Do not forget to film a video!

LEVEL UP

Have you tried seeing an entire picture while inside its frame? You can't. It is impossible. The very notion or thought detaches reality and the understanding of all that is human as well. The common interference of the "I am" before the word "possible" is incorrect. Although this notion has a fourth right stance on positive potentials it is misleading and a contradiction of truth. The truth is we are not "me" and anything "I" related is not "we" instead, but "me," and is rooted in falsehood. The correlation to positive results is just that; a correlative not a causation. Absence of evidence is not evidence of absence just as correlation is not causation and therefore, we must always widen the aperture and take our personal stance out of the equation. When we come full circle and stand above this thought we see truth that our pictures cannot be seen alone whilst standing chest puffed in our frame to find our *only* solution. Leveling up. The terminology or labeling may be new to you, but its context we're all too familiar. The parent, the friend, trusted advisor, mentor, big brother, the Socrates to your Plato or Plato to your Aristotle and your new mentor. Leveling up is mentoring up, think of it as humility in action. Forget the words and deep talk about knowing you that is for playing games in realization of consciousness, this is living in the act of mentorship. Ask yourself, are you open to growth? Does your heart beat to a different drummer? Not the idea of "I" and "me," but to a sovereign virtue of "we" and "us." Can you admit defeat and throw in your towel showing the humility of being an open human? These are the questions we ask before leveling up. This punch in the gut is the act before the action of fight or flight. Choose to run for your dreams and not to fight for your insecurities. Be humble and stand on the shoulders of giants to see your frame. Decide if your mind, heart, spirit and world view are in acceptance, for knowing that you do not know the answer is all that is important to know. Stop trying to see your own reflection and extend your hand for another to hand you their mirror. It is time to level up.

Leveling up is mentoring up, think of it as humility in action. – Level Up

_____

_____

_____

_____

_____

_____

_____

_____

_____

_____

_____

Do not forget to film a video!

URGENT HUMILITY

Barring down on you is a heavy burden, one of reckless endanger-
ment to all associates. It is the idea of importance. When we pride
ourselves on our own worth in respect to the value of another our
worth shines forth as less. However, this is the path for many lost
souls who society deems as "enlightened" or "righteous". Men,
women and children are considered the future of our humanity and
are weighed down by our biological, sociological and reckless nature;
self-aggrandizement and self-importance. Arguably, this is a product
of our social nurture and biological design. Our maker sometimes
unknown, but the results are clear. This stems from the effect of
causality or an endless striving for something. The result of this is
of perpetual instant gratification and selfish genes, in other words,
the comings of endless "me first "attitudes. When we look in the
mirror, we see ourselves, and when we listen to another, we hear our
own thoughts. We are deaf to criticism and of anything but acclaim.
When we speak our thoughts, we speak none other than those we
admire falsely, those we place on hierarchies, the Tsar's or the deities
we worship. Down on our knees we pray with our chin down, mind
closed tight, and eyes peeking up in hope for a blessing, but what
we miss is the central ingredient to being human and the urgency of
humility. This is the vaccine of the cancerous progeny of us and our
future selves which are one in the same to those who know nothing
of the cycle of life. The cyclical selfish smog of fear and resentment
like a wave on the naked shore is bludgeoning and disempowering
the ghouls, stupefied mass and followers causing rifts and inspiring
aimless drifting across the wilderness. This forest of deadwood we
may call corporate culture. The nesting ground for future devils of
the world with men who will be burdened with responsibility from
those who need not think what they have done grants permission
to be led. Non-leaders operate from desire and not as human, but
robotically maneuver within the malevolence of their predecessors.

After many cycles of self-importance and post haste, the generations following the initial flood of "self" and of "I" and of "me", we are here burdened by the weight of self-importance, and like no other time but of the historical past is lost forever while our own biological and social construct is not. We are selfish. We are self-proposed. We are important. This world is reckless, and our nature is burdened by our own reflection. Therefore, we must stop so we start living like never before. Living as human; human all too human.

This world is reckless, and our nature is burdened by our own reflection. – Urgent Humility

_____

_____

_____

_____

_____

_____

_____

_____

_____

_____

_____

_____

Do not forget to film a video!

Refer to page i for directions

Keep reading!
Keep writing!
Keep Filming!

DON'T FORGET TO FILM YOUR VIDEO!

Tag us when you're done!
Culture Matters
cultureunitesauthors

#thirtydaysofthought
#culturematters
#readwritespeak
#cultureunitesauthors

THINGS THAT ARE WRITTEN DOWN ARE OF IMPORTANCE

Writing in and of itself is not spectacular. After all, anyone can write. Since the dawn of man's ancestor's symbols have been scribed on the walls of remote caves all around the world. Regardless of origin these drawings have resembled underlying patterns. The commodity of this writing is so clear it begs a question- why? Well, what if unlike speech writing took deeper conviction? Let's put ourselves to the test, say something right now, go ahead, and make a statement about what you just read to a friend or a stranger nearby. Think about your interaction without being articulate at all, anyone listening nearby can use other senses like sight, context clues from your hands, eyes, body etc. and other sense in sound to hear your tone to formulate an understanding of what you are saying- why? Well, without testing we can presuppose to survive, meaning the drivers of our environment equip us to understand speech relatively at ease. What could differ in terms of writing? I dare say everything. Think about grammar, grammar is the solution to those other senses being lost in translation when pen touches parchment. Without all the necessary tools required to imagine what the speaker, or writer imagines the audience is lost. If the audience or social tribe is lost, they die! This is life or death; grammar is life or death. Pedagogy is beginning and ending, coming and going and listening or drifting off. When it comes down to writing we are forced through ours and the psychology of our audience to be more articulate. We must align our thoughts clearly to make what we see in our imagination clear to the reader. The readers lack the visual, audio and other sense receptors necessary to understand and therefore, we must use grammar and other written laws eloquently to deliver a coherent message; writing culture matters. All these tools are not biologically fluid or auspicious like our tonality and our body when we speak. The societal norms of everyday communication picked up in adolescence and utilized for basic survival bestow upon us the latter. These important variables in writing are conscious and learned therefore they take energy. It is this energy explosion that destroys our old self and rebuilds our new form better, grander and wiser whilst enhancing our readers simultaneously. Energy is calories and calories are life. Each time we invest in articulating our thoughts to raise the awareness of our readership we raise the awareness of our metaphorical tribe, humans. Things we write down are important in raising the social consciousness beginning with the idea and ending with your words through a pen. Each generation basks in the articulated imagination of the prior generation through the writing of the cave man we have modeled. From the confines of the library we will rise. Be great my readers and revel in the development of our reality of which relies on the written word. Things that are important are always written down. What do you feel compelled to write now?

From the confines of the library we will rise. – Things That Are Written Down are of Importance

_____

_____

_____

_____

_____

_____

_____

_____

_____

_____

_____

Do not forget to film a video!

THE FINAL HOUR

When the walls are closing in on you from every direction it's easy to stop breathing. Your lungs close tight and there is just enough room for one breath every so often to creep in and keep you from passing out. The asphyxiation continues, and your eyelids weigh heavy, before the lights dim out a brief thought floods your mind, "don't quit". Sometimes all it takes before failure is a sudden reminder, the voice in the back of your head whispering power into your ear. This quiet power comes from you and no one else. The future lies in your head; this is your dream and no one else's. Failure only comes into existence when you say no to that voice and drown under the pressure of those walls closing in. They are made up of the people who count on you, tasks under assignment with due dates. These walls that entrap you are the ventures you started and the promises you made. They are all the weight of responsibilities thrust upon you. They are the catch 22 of this dream we call success and with every dream there lies its final hour, just before we wakeup. The final hour is the thunder before the rainbow, it's the hell before any heaven, and it's the waiting room before the doctor's office 211 degrees closer to success and just one hour from living it. Just one degree from reveling in its boiling water the cesspool for all life started with a boil. The cosmological or macro representation of you has biological, psychological and neurological counterparts, they all started with a boil and one degree away from heaven; our creation. Your future is standing before you and you may not even notice. Simply due to those four walls closing on you and the invisible architecture of survival, fear, doubt, and lonesome needs to be pushed through by you. Focus and be sure to remember that you don't need anyone to breath for you, just breath. It is the final hour.

Sometimes all it takes before failure is sudden reminder, the voice in the back of your head whispering power into your ear. – The Final Hour

_____

_____

_____

_____

_____

_____

_____

_____

_____

_____

_____

_____

_____

Do not forget to film a video!

THE MAN WHO SPEAKS, SAYS NOTHING

The man, who speaks, says nothing. A man of competence in speech and of a genealogical pedigree is predisposed of such talents, but unfortunately indoctrinated into self-gratification, almost always. "Oh, woe unto us" says, the simpletons, the crowd, the mass and ignorant many. We are plagued with power in the hands of men who deserve nothing of praise. These men and their raw talents left to the devices of happenstance; probability of genes and talents unearned. "Oh, the drudgery" - left unto our sheer mass of fearful followers, and pragmatics hell bent off mediocrity, and average habituation. Without conscious recall we are but simultaneously building up those who do not deserve it. Those who do not respect themselves enough to have the praise they receive, and then we develop their socially constructed-hollow value. We, the masses, the deserved and the shackled fearful spectators place the speakers on this pedestal, and crop unto them this painted veil they wear ever so promptly. This mask of the "fake alpha", this lie they tell themselves as we listen, eagerly and in awe. These men in fact say nothing. What is the cost to us? The onlooker...life itself.

To put plainly, it is in sight for all who digest this clear-cut dissertation of aggravation toward these cowardly men with hollow hearts, weak minds and sub-primal understanding. Men who focus their aims with stature and status. Figures of our socially constructed regards based on nothing but smoke and mirrors. The unfortunate effect of causality due to the collocation of industrialization, materializations and informative individuation misinterpreted and mis-aligned all in happenstance, an age of abundance and of lack thereof. The lack of confidence, intrinsic value, the smog of political correctness corrupting those whom have a voice, a heart and the mind to yield power but are not in presence with their truth to stand up and shout! The men, women and children who have value to give something to share and must speak! These people, the ones of whom earned the right to speak, the ones of whom win the label of human and all it entails. Love, courage, empathy and power. Real Power. Mind Power. Vocal Power. Written Power. These humans do not speak, but those who are not just, who are cogs in the metaphorical wheel of materialism, hedonism and bureaucracy. These cogs are spinning out of control with the wheel of falsehood, where lack of meaning and an abundance of betrayal arrive. Ignorance in motion with a misguided solidarity, and a mis-aligned culture. These ghoul's standup in their conviction whether true or false, and they raise their vocals for the crowds to hear and I say, "blasphemy!" Shame on them for their ignorance, nothing but the walking dead, and even still, shame on you for your lack of decisiveness. Shame on you for your silent voice. I wrote this not in contempt, but in contemplation. I speak out not in condemnation, but in emancipation. I finish my piece, in peace, not in ambivalence, but in revelation. One truth holds true, and that is true of progress. We live, we breath, we speak... even in the word, transcribed, we bring value...and if upon reflection someone passes this note and they CAN make a change- then it was all worth it. My reader, my friend, and my speaker, I implore you to read between the lines and find your footing, aid and abet the conversation by being brave and speaking up. It is your duty, responsibility and my conviction to rattle you. Why? Because we must, I know I am- for too many speakers speak... and when they do, we listen, but they say nothing...

My reader, my friend, and my speaker, I implore you to read between the lines and find your footing, aid and abet the conversation by being brave and speaking up. It is your duty, responsibility and my conviction to rattle you. – The Man Who Speaks, Says Nothing

_____

_____

_____

_____

_____

_____

_____

_____

_____

_____

_____

_____

Do not forget to film a video!

Refer to page i for directions

Keep reading!
Keep writing!
Keep Filming!

DON'T FORGET TO FILM YOUR VIDEO!

Tag us when you're done!
 Culture Matters
 cultureunitesauthors

#thirtydaysofthought
#culturematters
#readwritespeak
#cultureunitesauthors

STEPPING INTO YOUR LIGHT

For 30 days a commitment was made, the target was set and our being stretched through its maximum elasticity. The scope of our potential has been met, even if just for 30 days. A cleansing of our mind, our body and our soul has taken place. The mind purified by new thoughts. Imaginative possibilities have been plucked from the invisible layer of nothingness nested between our minds and the universes infinite beyond. A stadium of possibility lies before us. We are the singer, songwriter and maestro of our symphony, pen in hand and a hidden scribe of sorts has been evoked. Heavy is the pen straining in thought, the burden of our inner conflict grows cancerous the longer it bares on our mind and taught if the hand wrapped around our sword, the pen, yearning for bloodshed, its ink pouring out of the spout and not yet drained. This key is, the soul opening its gateway to all new ideas under the gravity of interpretation and innovations falling off the man, the woman, the child, in deep suggestive thought. It is cleansing in mind, body and soul to invest time, caloric output and mental fortitude in such a task and yet these acts of reading, reflecting, and pulling streams of imagination are what we may call genius, your genius. Creation out of only the surface and articulation into the vortex is to read, imagine, transcribe, articulate and evoke your truth with the common tongue. Genius can have no greater fruit than that of creation. Life itself lies in between what is imagined and what is manifested. Life is itself the purest of genius and what is genius? Genius is what lies between recognition of pattern and imagination. Genius is recognition of pattern and imagination juxtaposed by manic action until manifestation. Genius lies within us, it is in fact the "genie" within us and all of life's answers are found within the confines of our inner world, but only after the discovery of every feat of our outer worlds and thus we must read, write and speak to accomplish this mission of self-discovery. The meaning of our lives will only grow as wide and as deep as the caverns of our need, will no walls shorten its width and no ceiling limiting its lid; our universal mind the collective unconscious. It's but an uninhibited, unfiltered funnel of truth convicting a master, but solely due to our decision to master our mind, body and soul. Mastery is the decision to pursue the latter. We do that, we start this journey of exploration of the infinite with our daily tasks to read, write and speak. The more we refine our daily to do's the closer we come to our personal power. The fortress of hell surrounding us is our limiting belief that will fall, and our hidden but everlasting truth will shine through. Our being will have no bearing on this physical plane and no obstacle but the person we see in the mirror can hinder our growth but only when we read, write and speak daily may our power soar unencumbered. We are our own superman or superwoman if we choose it to be. As for the faint of heart the man, woman and child unsure of their place in this world and unsure of themselves, other powers yet unknown to them, and their ability to read, write and speak will make them their own superhero. For that, we share with you one word, "persist." The individual inside the frame may not be able to see their power but only see that life's mountain has different views from each peak. We may all be on a journey together and on the same mountain simultaneously in our time, but at which peak, and under which view we have no way of discerning. Each of us has our own peak, summit edge to perch ourselves on and interpret from to draw on or view and paint our canvas of life with the tools we have available to us. There is no secret here for we are all on different slopes of the mountain, so we do repeat, "Persist," because it may not be today, it may not be tomorrow but someday soon or on your days last sunrise you may have a change in view. How can we gravitate to never see our truest sunrise? We don't persist to give up on life's journey as that is the definite guarantee to never be at peace and to never discover our truth, our power and empower those around us. If you are this man, woman or child then that is you, that is your path. If you cross a man, woman or child on that path look both ways acknowledge them and then keep on your path. Your path as empowered in self is clear and that of love, courage and discovery.

Stay true to our vision, to inspire every man, woman and child to take responsibility to read, write and speak every day. Do this simply by being your true self; empowered. Stay true to the mission and do this by taking responsibility for yourself. Take heed of every word you speak. Take heed of every thought you have. Be open to new ideas and form an agreement with only one fact: that facts of the now will be facts of what was as soon as the new becomes now. Facts are material observations of matter and matter's relationship to culture contrasts beautifully to appear designed regardless of any absolute truth. One influences the other and the other influences the other back- it is cyclical. Things, societies, and life evolve from this relationship. Flow with life as water flows in the creek. Stay true to your values and let them guide the facts. Be true to your "daily musts" and you will grow as life grows because all must change, all must die but being and legacy is forever. Read, write and speak and every fact will be heard for you, all will collaborate with you and life itself will mold for you. Allow your evolution so the facts of your life evolve because your culture matters.

Mysterious Mentor-
Dedication

He is no sophist and he is not a wordsmith. He is no myth buster, the devil not his master nor an almighty his maker. He is just and unjust all in one. The pen is his bayonet, the parchment is his rifle, each bullet a thought in his mind with an endless armory filled with ammunition. He is what is a soul of man and a feeling of a woman. He is one with himself; his power unmatched. He is our mystery man one among the mass, one in a billion and a symbol of conflicted genius. He grappled with the dark and brought forth his light, misinterpretations and all. His genius expounded through provocative prose riddled with harsh candor and explained with an aphoristic style is unmatched and unparalleled. He is the demonstration of an outlier and the habituation of individualism. This man is our martyr without recognition. He was for us and against us and from his mountains peak spoke what only the deaf could hear that our mystery man lives on within us as our voice of reason. He is _our_ will to power and our _lighthouse_.

A Chance to win a three-day mentorship with Culture Unites Authors, Tyler Wagner and Jay Doran! ($50,000 value!)

Here is what you have to do:

1. *Post your favorite excerpt from the book*
2. *Post the mystery mentor excerpt page above with your mystery answers*

Dedication: A.W.

Without constant flux, change and open borders unto which energy and love can flow, life perishes. That is not a threat in respect to you, for as an ocean fills abundant and plentiful in its duty to pour into the many streams it fills, those streams also must be open to receive its grandeur. You were, are, have been and will continue to be an overflow in that initial stream that by material, physical, and universal law becomes an ocean. This is not theory, this is law and for that, you are great. We are blessed to have you and to pour into you. Our friend and no matter what course life's borders take your stream, your ocean, this oceanic source called, Culture Matters, will continue to pour love into you. Keep dreaming, stay open, continue to be curious, continue to discover yourself, and continue to observe as you do, for I know no other as I know you. It's an honor to watch you grow by telling your truth. We dedicate a page to you, our friend, Antwan- love you.

Dedication- A.V.

You saw what was not seen. You thought of me in my utmost when it had still been unseen. The time has passed quietly while we have plotted two souls only a moment apart in this dance called life and all along inseparable and aligned by trust. Trust is the lasso non-descript, but abundant and interpretable by the one thing that matters to me, your belief. When no one believed in me, you did, when everyone decided to leave, you stayed, and at times of adversity you held tight. When I crumbled, you stood tall and strong-willed leading our ship of, Culture Matters. You are my friend, my family, my quarterback, and the game would not be in play if not for your faith. The belief in the cause, a love for its maker, and vision of what is unseen even to me. I dedicate this book to you along with a special place in my soul. For as long as I live, I owe you a debt of gratitude for believing in me when no one else did. Thank you.

Dedication: J.S.

The darkness overcame his soul, overstepped all logic, and fought his heart with an omen of fear and anxiety that cut so deep that no aid could vaccinate his self-loathing, or so he thought. Then you came with wind ablaze, eyes wide, an open heart and the personal vigor to overlook the dark surrounding him to see his light. The genius within him and the articulated thought we are all capable of but do not normally uncover. You guided him to his beginning. For that patience, persistence and passion for the stranger at a bar that fateful night it was you who inspired him, gave him courage, listened when he wept and did not allow him to give up on writing. With that, our readers consume the mind of a tattered soul and a bellowing heart, only for them to become who they are capable being; the genius they do not yet know, their true self, the men or women their mirror holds hostage. The writing started with you. I, the writer am him, and in this dedication, I bless you and Thirty Days of Thought as it started with you. The patient guide, Jenna, thank you.

Dedication to the Doubters

Love is the secret weapon. Why? Because the essence of what composes love is the same energy force split to combust the atomic bomb. The atom is representation of a source to a source, that of energy. Energy flows through all regardless of labeling, non-judgmental, non-bigoted, inept of racism, non-conforming to gossip but adept in bringing everything together, that is love. Unlike our visible source, the sun, love is unable to be seen literally, but only figuratively or syllogistically due to our impact or feeling. We, the collective mass, whether in hate or in love are impacted, and for that, only love is in my heart for the doubters as it must for there ever to be hope. After all, human culture matters most and if we are ever to be one and unify under one vision and mission through a purpose worth living, we must believe in love. I dedicate this to our doubters with love in our hearts and through our love, we say, I love you.

DEDICATION TO BELIEVERS

Your light was, is and will be bright no matter how much darkness surrounds you. I strive to earn your love for me and the light you shine for us at Culture Matters. Tears dropping gently leaving no guard up or wall overbearing on the discussion, I write this in pain and conflict but with smiles, wide eyes and an external loving embrace. We fight this everlasting fight for you and through your light we have the support, the strength, the mind, and personal power to condemn evil and utilize the dark maximizing all human potential. We believe when people read, write and speak every day they develop love for themselves and others. Through our mission, we win every day no matter what is said, thought or done. We shine bright and it is you, the reader and our believer that we do it through. With that we dedicate this to you, and grace you with our truth. Thank you. You are a dancing star.

CULTURE MATTERS

* Belief, Purpose, Goal, Vision, Mission *

Our Belief

We believe when people read to think, write to develop, listen to understand and speak to let go they develop love for themselves and others.

Our Purpose

To help people uncover their genius!

Our Goal

To make curiosity cool!

Our Vision

Human culture is open, curious and focused on creating our future.

Our Mission

To read, write, speak and inspire others to do the same!

CULTURE MATTERS

Values

Collaboration

Give first, intend to help, get started today.

Unique

Education is finding the answer within.

Learned

The more you learn, the more you earn.

Trustworthy

Trust in yourself so you can trust others.

Unstoppable

Your losses don't matter, because you'll win in the end, never give up.

Reserved

Listen to understand not to reply.

Enthusiastic

Convey love passionately.

---

*M*ove

Make it happen, do it now.

---

*A*spire

Aspire to inspire, before you expire.

---

*T*winkle

Turn that frown upside down, laugh a lot.

---

*T*alk

Always talk to strangers, every person has a story to be heard.

---

*E*ase

Slow down to speed up. Take a deep breath and follow your plan.

---

*R*esponsibility

Don't expect to be hugged first. Take initiative and love with a hug.

---

*S*unshine

Remember you are light. Read, write and speak daily and unlimited power will flow through you enough to light up any room.

The End.

**YOU ARE NOT ONLY WRITING YOUR
BOOK– YOU ARE WRITING YOUR LIFE
CULTURE . UNITES . AUTHORS**

The Culture Collective

Book 1: The Liar Lid: Obstacle

Book 2: Thirty Days of Thought: Workout

Book 3: The Utility Journal: Gymnasium

Book 4: The Deficit: Power Source

Book 5: The Container: Avatar

Book 6: The Culture Puzzle: Group

Book 7: Fifty-Two Weeks of Thought: Lifestyle